JESUS THE ETERNAL SON

Jesus the Eternal Son

Answering Adoptionist Christology

Michael F. Bird

WILLIAM B. EERDMANS PUBLISHING COMPANY

GRAND RAPIDS, MICHIGAN

Wm. B. Eerdmans Publishing Co.
2140 Oak Industrial Drive N.E., Grand Rapids, Michigan 49505
www.eerdmans.com

26 25 24 23 22 21 20 19 18 17   1 2 3 4 5 6 7 8 9 10

ISBN 978-0-8028-7506-8

Library of Congress Cataloging-in-Publication Data

Names: Bird, Michael F., author.
Title: Jesus the eternal son : answering adoptionist Christology /
    Michael F. Bird.
Description: Grand Rapids : Eerdmans Publishing Co., 2017. | Includes bibliographical
    references and index.
Identifiers: LCCN 2017010013 | ISBN 9780802875068 (pbk. : alk. paper)
Subjects: LCSH: Jesus Christ—Person and offices. | Jesus Christ—Divinity. | Adoptionism.
Classification: LCC BT203 .B536 2017 | DDC 232/.8—dc23
    LC record available at https://lccn.loc.gov/2017010013

For the three Craigs

Craig Evans
Craig Keener
Craig Blomberg

Table of Contents

CONTENTS

Foreword

For some time now, early Christology has been the subject of intense and lively debate. The result has been important and fresh research. "What did the earliest Christians really think about Jesus?" is a question on the minds of many people. Did early believers in Christ really worship him as a divine figure? Or did they think of Jesus as a merely human figure whom God had exalted to a position of great eminence? Was the earliest Christology to which we have access already very high, as the scholarly trend known as early high Christology has argued? A wide range of scholars now think so; Michael Bird is prominent among them. However, many scholars still defend an older model of the evolution of Christology from what has often been called an adoptionist view toward an understanding of Jesus as the divine Son of God incarnate, which was perhaps only reached toward the end of the New Testament period, in the Gospel of John. There have been important recent challenges to early high Christology, some of which offer relatively new suggestions about the ideas available in the context of early Christianity that could have provided a model for Christian interpretation of Jesus. Bird's book engages with some of those ideas, especially with the ones about the deification of Roman emperors and other prominent human beings. Such proposals build on a long scholarly tradition of reading certain key New Testament texts as evidence for an early view of Jesus as a man whom God adopted as his son, whether at his resurrection or at his baptism.

This book is very welcome because, surprisingly, the idea of divine sonship has not received the attention it deserves in the discussion of early high Christology. Yet it has a central role in the New Testament as a whole. It embodies the sense that Jesus did not come to be divine but came from God in the first place. It is the key notion that ties together his pre-existence, his earthly life, and his exaltation in continuity. It is the way that early Christians came to be able to think of Jesus's relationship to God his Father as an inner divine reality. It functions both exclusively (designating Jesus's unique relation to his Father) and also inclusively, as the relationship to God that Jesus enables believers to share. As such, it belongs to both a Christological and a soteriological category.

So did it all start with the view that divine sonship was a status that the man Jesus gained by merit and divine appointment? Bird—although he allows for variation and gradually clearer definition in early Christology— finds that there is no evidence at all for adoptionism in the early period. He tackles the texts that have so often been read in an adoptionist way and shows, I think convincingly, that this cannot plausibly be the original meaning. In his search for the origins of adoptionism, Bird moves into the second century and finds what he is looking for only at the very end of that century. Far from being considered the earliest Christology, adoptionism now appears to be actually a very late divergence from the main current of Christian thinking on the subject. Instead of being a view that preceded any ontological thinking about Jesus's relation to God, it turns out to be a view designed to protect an ontology of divine nature that could not accommodate incarnation within it. Many New Testament scholars will likely be surprised by this conclusion, but many patristic scholars, I suspect, will not.

I am happy to commend this learned, cogent, and significant book.

RICHARD BAUCKHAM

Preface

This volume is the result of preparation for a public dialogue about the divinity of Jesus held at the Greer-Heard Point-Counter-Point forum at New Orleans Baptist Theological Seminary in February 2016. Participants included Bart Ehrman, Jennifer Knust, Dale Martin, Larry Hurtado, Simon Gathercole, and me.

As I began preparing my talk on Jesus and adoptionism, it soon became apparent to me that a lot of what was being said about the origins of christological adoptionism was incorrect. What is more, in response to all this, it soon became clear that I had more to communicate than I had time to speak. What I wrote for the Greer-Heard debate was too substantial for a lecture or even for a journal article on the subject and more suited in length for a short, sharp, and provocative volume on the topic. So here we are!

I first gained interest in the topic of adoptionism after noticing that many scholars simply assume rather than argue the point that the earliest Christology of the primitive church was adoptionistic. The only evidence mustered is more often than not a footnote to the same cohort of scholars, usually John Knox and James D. G. Dunn, but without ever critically appraising their theses. My own suspicion was that, to quote George Gershwin, "it ain't necessarily so." I would not for a moment deny the diversity of portraits of Jesus that emerged in the early church, some emphasizing his humanity. However, in my reading of the sources a mature adoptionism is a second-century phenomenon. The first real and tangible advocates were the Theodotians.

I would like to thank Bob Stewart for inviting me again to the Greer-Heard forum. I would also like to thank my fellow participants in the discussion and those who made the event possible. The "Nawleans" hospitality and collegiality was outstanding! I love being able to say that I have had blackened crawfish from down on the bayou!

Several friends read over parts of the manuscript and offered comments for which I am most grateful. Joshua Jipp, once the apprentice now the master, was great with corrections, affirmations, and suggestions. So too did Matthew Bates have a close read of the manuscript and point out to me certain ways to enhance it. Con Campbell answered a hairy Greek question for me. My colleague Scott Harrower made a few learned comments too. Christoph Heilig helped track down a few German works that were inaccessible to me. Michael Peppard provided some crucial feedback in making sure I represented his view correctly. He also pushed back on several vital details. An anonymous reviewer supplied by Eerdmans made several pointed suggestions as to how to improve the quality of the argumentation and readability of the book, for which I am most grateful. Also, the Ridley librarians Ruth Millard and Alison Foster ordered several volumes that I needed to read in order to complete the book. Thanks also go to John Schoer for ably compiling the indexes.

This volume is dedicated to three guys called Craig, scholars whose work on Jesus and the Gospels has taught me much and inspired me to excellence in my own writing. First, I read Craig Blomberg's textbooks on *Jesus and the Gospels* and *Interpreting the Parables* back in theological college. I then had the honor of meeting Blomberg in person when he came to lecture at Moore Theological College in Sydney back in 2004. Since then I have regularly enjoyed catching up with Blomberg at conferences. I have always felt like he was a kindred spirit, and his academic work still teaches me much. Second, it has been great collaborating with Craig Evans and getting to know him better now that we are colleagues at Houston Baptist University, where I am an adjunct research professor. Evans is a very personable scholar, and I continue to benefit from his writings. They set the gold standard for evangelical scholarship on the Gospels. Third, Craig Keener's reputation precedes him. Like most seminary students since the 1990s, I have long benefited from Keener's volumes, especially his massive commentaries. I have been in awe of his encyclopedic grasp of first-century sources. I first met Keener while browsing over his Matthew commentary at the SBL book stalls. Since then I have had the privilege of personal friendship and professional collaboration with him, and even the pleasure of hosting him in Australia. In sum, anyone wanting to learn what careful and disciplined study of the Gospels looks like in practice really should consult this "Craig's List" of venerable scholars. If I were to receive a slight portion of their *genius*, I know I would be a much better teacher and researcher. May peace and grace be theirs in abundance!

Abbreviations

AB	Anchor Bible
ANF	*Ante-Nicene Fathers*
BBR	*Bulletin for Biblical Research*
BibInt	Biblical Interpretation Series
CBQ	*Catholic Biblical Quaterly*
CurBS	*Currents in Research: Biblical Studies*
EKKNT	Evangelisch-katholischer Kommentar zum Neuen Testament
ExpTim	*Expository Times*
HThKNT	Herders Theologischer Kommentar zum Neuen Testament
HTR	*Harvard Theological Review*
ICC	International Critical Commentary
IHR	*The International History Review*
ITQ	*Irish Theological Quarterly*
JAJ	*Journal of Ancient Judaism*
JBL	*Journal of Biblical Literature*
JSHJ	*Journal for the Study of the Historical Jesus*
JSJSup	Supplements to the Journal for the Study of Judaism
JSNT	*Journal for the Study of New Testament*
JSNTSup	Journal for the Study of New Testament Supplement Series
JTI	*Journal for Theological Interpretation*

LCL	Loeb Classical Library
LNTS	The Library of New Testament Studies
NovT	*Novum Testamentum*
NovTSup	Supplements to Novum Testamentum
NPNF[1]	*Nicene and Post-Nicene Fathers*, Series 1
NPNF[2]	*Nicene and Post-Nicene Fathers*, Series 2
NTS	*New Testament Studies*
RBL	*Review of Biblical Literature*
SBT	Studies in Biblical Theology
SNTSMS	Society for New Testament Studies Monograph Series
TynBul	*Tyndale Bulletin*
TS	*Theological Studies*
VCSup	Supplements to Vigiliae Christianae
WBC	World Biblical Commentary
WMANT	Wissenschaftliche Monographien zum Alten und Neuen Testament
WUNT	Wissenschaftliche Untersuchungen zum Neuen Testament

CHAPTER 1

Christology and Christian Origins

The Birth of Christology

It is very difficult to provide a comprehensive description of how early Christian beliefs about Jesus emerged in a way that adequately summarizes the many contexts, texts, artifacts, and complexities that were formative for those Christian beliefs.[1] At the risk of simplification, I would suggest that early Christologies emerged as the attempt to express, in belief and devotion, what the earliest Christ-believers thought God had revealed in the life, passion, resurrection, and exaltation of Jesus of Nazareth. In addition, there was a palpable need to make sense of what they had experienced of Jesus in their own communal and interior religious life. Reflection on Jesus's prophetic career and the events of the first Easter—in addition to practices like prayer, worship, healing, visionary experiences, and charismatic phenomena—fostered a set of shared convictions about Jesus among adherents of the primitive churches. Core to those convictions was not only that Jesus was God's agent, but that Jesus was to be identified with God and with God's activities in the world—at least in some sense.[2] Thus, early Christologies were driven by a mixture of ideational

1. For a good summary of recent debates see Andrew Chester, "High Christology—Whence, When and Why?" *Early Christianity* 2 (2011): 22–50.
2. The notion of Jesus as part of the "divine identity" was put forward by Richard Bauckham, *Jesus and the God of Israel: God Crucified and Other Studies on the New Testament's Christology of Divine Identity* (Grand Rapids: Eerdmans, 2009), esp. 1–59. What

factors (beliefs, propositions, and cognitive frameworks) and experiential events (rituals, devotional practices, and sensations of divine presence and power). This led to the creations of narratives and propositions that attempted to answer a double-sided question: (1) Who is Jesus? and (2) Who is God in light of the memory of Jesus and the continuing experience of Jesus? This is where Christology began.

On the question of Jesus's identity, a simple glance through the New Testament shows that Jesus was described in many ways: as a miracle-working prophet, a new Davidic Messiah, the mysterious "Son of Man," the pre-existent Son of God, a priestly agent with divine power, a heavenly figure with angelic qualities, the personification of divine wisdom, God's messianic κύριος, and the divine Logos made flesh. Scholars often mistakenly assume that these beliefs were mutually exclusive and that one view could only be held by one community at any one time. It is more likely, however, that assertions about Jesus's identity swirled around early Christian networks, no doubt competing for consensus.[3] These ideas converged

Bauckham means by "divine identity" is "who" God is rather than "what" he is, specifically, the revelation of his name YHWH and his relationship to the whole of reality as creator and ruler. But this approach has been criticized by others. For example, James D. G. Dunn, *Did the First Christians Worship Jesus? The New Testament Evidence* (London: SPCK, 2010), 141–44, wonders whether "identity" is displacing the historical term "person" and whether "identity" runs the risk of modalism. Dunn thinks it might be better to describe Jesus as a person with divine functions, a description that has precedents in the Wisdom tradition. Matthew Bates, *The Birth of the Trinity* (Oxford: Oxford University Press, 2015), 24–25, is similarly concerned that "divine identity" de-emphasizes the ontic relationship between the Father and the Son and that the model needlessly displaces the more helpful category of personhood. J. R. Daniel Kirk, *A Man Attested by God: The Human Jesus of the Synoptic Gospels* (Grand Rapids: Eerdmans, 2016), 174, warns that being identified with God is not the same as being identified as God. He notes that Judaism is filled with ideal human figures identified with God but without encroaching on God's unique identity. In defense of Bauckham's thesis of divine identity, see Crispin H. T. Fletcher-Louis, *Jesus Monotheism*, vol. 1 of *Christological Origins: The Emerging Consensus and Beyond* (Eugene, OR: Wipf & Stock, 2015), 14, who says that: "Time and again we find divine *action* or *functions* ascribed to Christ in a way that now makes sense if Christ belongs within the divine identity and if he fully participates in the divine nature" (italics original). On the whole idea of human and divine identities, see Nina Henrichs-Tarasenkova, *Luke's Christology of Divine Identity*, LNTS 542 (London: T&T Clark, 2016), 26–88.

3. Several examples can suffice of early competition to hammer out Jesus's identity in the early church. John the Elder wrote letters in the vicinity of Ephesus around

and coalesced into a constellation of common convictions about Christ among the proto-orthodox churches of the second century.[4]

---

the 90s CE contending with denials that Jesus was the Messiah (1 John 2:22, reflecting Jewish criticism) or else denials that he came in the flesh (1 John 4:2; 2 John 7, reflecting a Hellenization of Christology). Ignatius, the Syrian bishop of Antioch (ca. 110 CE) similarly warned against "atheists," those who "mix Jesus Christ with themselves" (*Trall.* 6.2; 10.1) and have a docetic Christology (*Eph.* 7.1–9.1; *Trall.* 8.1–11.2; *Magn.* 11.1; *Smyrn.* 1.1–7.2) and against judaizing Gentile Christians who have an inadequate account of Jesus (*Phild.* 6.1–2; *Magn.* 9.1–2). Other second-century bishops, like Polycarp of Smyrna (*Phil.* 7.1–2) and Serapion of Antioch, also dealt with the docetist controversy (Eusebius, *Hist. eccl.* 6.12). The author of the Epistle of Barnabas (early second century CE) indicates the relative insufficiency of treating Jesus as a mere "son of man" or even as a "son of David" when his true identity is better described as the Son of God, who is foreshadowed in the OT, and revealed to have come in the flesh in the new covenant (Barn. 12.8–12). In the Gospel of Thomas (early to mid-second century CE) there is a scene where Jesus asks three of his disciples who he is like and they respond in various ways, with Simon Peter answering "a righteous angel," Matthew "a wise philosopher," and Thomas pleading an inability to describe Jesus (Gos. Thom. 13). The Testimony of Truth, a gnostic tractate from the late second century CE, denigrates those who call themselves Christians but are ignorant of Christ and human destiny (Testim. Truth 9.31–32). In the Revelation of Adam (a Gnostic writing from the first to fourth centuries CE), Adam describes thirteen erroneous views of the "Illuminator of Knowledge" by correlating them with thirteen kingdoms. The kingdoms described in Apoc. Adam 7.1–52 include alternative gnostic views largely related to the manner of Jesus's coming, but the seventh kingdom looks like a cross between angel-Christology and adoptionism (Apoc. Adam 7.24–26), while the thirteenth kingdom very probably echoes a Logos Christology (Apoc. Adam 7.45–48). The longer recension of the letters of Ignatius (fourth century CE) includes an interpolated tirade in *Phild.* 6.1 against several Christologies espoused within Judaism, Gnosticism, Ebionism, Docetism, Encraticism, and Apollinarianism. A most notable example of christological diversity is that there were three Christian teachers in the city of Rome ca. 150 CE who each had different views on the birth of Jesus: Justin said he was born of a virgin (*1 Apol.* 1.21, 33–34; *Dial.* 23, 43, 45, 66–68), Marcion is alleged to have said that Jesus had no birth at all (Irenaeus, *Haer.* 4.33.2; Tertullian, *Marc.* 3.11; 4.7; also espoused by Saturnius according to Irenaeus, *Haer.* 1.24.2), and Valentinus claimed that Jesus passed through Mary like water through a pipe and had a body composed of psychic and cosmic elements (Tertullian, *Carn. Chr.* 1, 6, 15; Ps-Tertullian, *Haer.* 4; Irenaeus, *Haer.* 3.11.3; Clement of Alexandria, *Exc.* 59).

4. Martin Hengel, "Christological Titles in Early Christianity," in *The Messiah*, ed. James H. Charlesworth (Minneapolis: Fortress, 1992), 443, comments: "The comparison of the three hymns in the Johannine Prologue, the Letter to the Hebrews and the Letter to the Philippians shows, first of all, that christological thinking between 50 and 100 CE *was much more unified in its basic structure* than New Testament research, in part

The raw materials for proto-orthodoxy and, indeed, later Nicene Orthodoxy reside in the teachers—and their communities—who wrote the documents that formed the New Testament. While christological claims do not appear to have been the most contested matters of first-century churches, we find indications already in the New Testament that certain aspects of Jesus's person and work were regarded as intrinsic and defining for certain communities.[5] That is most likely because tinkering with Jesus meant tinkering with the type of salvation he provided, which in turn undermined a particular expression of group identity. Thus, "Who is Jesus?" is important because it is directly connected to "What has God done for us through Jesus?" and "Who are we?" What one thinks of Jesus will determine what one has received from him and who his followers should understand themselves to be in the divine plan. There is little wonder that Jesus's identity became a central, albeit flexible, fixture of the early church. It explains why we detect in the first generations of the church a number of repeated titles for Jesus being used—such as Messiah, Lord, Savior, Son of Man, and Son of God—within a common kerygmatic narrative centered upon his life, death, resurrection, ascension, and future return. Early narrations of the story of Jesus described it as a divinely orchestrated sequence that results in salvation, a salvation in which Jesus played, continues to play, and will yet play, a key role. In light of this, it is clear that conceptions of Jesus's identity were not determined by abstract speculations, but by his specific role in the deliverance wrought by God and its associated benefits for his followers. We can affirm that among many early Christ-believers there was broad and near-immediate unity on two key christological ideas: (1) identification of Jesus *with* the God of Israel (in a very intense albeit ambiguous sense); and (2) identification of Jesus of Nazareth as the risen and exalted Lord Jesus Christ (fostering a unity between Jesus's earthly career and his exalted status). These ideas, I submit, were the germinal seeds of christological orthodoxy.[6]

---

at least, has maintained" (italics original). In addition, I would add that Luke–Acts and the letters of Ignatius show an immediate synthesis of Synoptic, Pauline, and perhaps even Johannine Christologies into a recognizable unity-in-diversity.

5. See 2 Cor 11:4; 1 John 2:22; 4:2; 2 John 7.

6. Cf. James D. G. Dunn, *Unity and Diversity in the New Testament: An Inquiry into the Character of Earliest Christianity*, 3rd ed. (London: SCM, 2006), 369; Larry W.

It was of course not all smooth sailing from Nazareth to Nicea. Complicating factors included varied presentations of Jesus's person in light of diverse interpretations of Israel's Scriptures, the struggle of the Judean and trans-Jordan churches to find legitimation for their messianic faith within common Judaism (pre-70 CE), and then antagonism with proto-rabbinic Judaism (post-70 CE). In addition, by the middle of the first century we already see the first phase of an extended encounter with Hellenism and its philosophies, the influence of Jewish and Greco-Roman categories for divine agents, and the adaptation of the Jesus story to various Hellenistic literary genres. Then follows the multiplication and dissemination of Christian writings, ranging from "other" Gospels to anti-heretical tracts, and an increasing diversification of the churches geographically, linguistically, and theologically. Even imperial politics in the third and fourth centuries shaped christological debates. All of this fashioned the christological language and devotional patterns of the early church.

Resultantly, we cannot speak of a single monolithic Christology of the early church, but neither can we settle for postulating an endless variety of Christologies that were all mutually exclusive and proportionately distributed across the early church, each with equal claims to validity. Therefore, rather than refer to a single and uniform "early Christology," I prefer to speak of "early christologizing," with various expressions of Jesus's identity gradually clustering together, becoming fused through the sharing of texts, the development of a common lexicon, shared hermeneutical strategies, and common rituals. The upshot was that a cohesive mode of discourse and mutually recognized patterns of worship gradually emerged. Concurrently, seemingly incongruent beliefs and practices began to be pushed to the margins when they did not meet with consensus or find reciprocation in the burgeoning church communities.

These incongruent Christologies—later labeled as "heresies"—were regarded as invalid portrayals of Jesus. The Jesus described by a growing collection of fringe groups either could not be squared with existing be-

---

Hurtado, *One God, One Lord: Early Christian Devotion and Ancient Jewish Monotheism* (Philadelphia: Fortress, 1988), 116.

liefs or else was simply unrecognizable to others. These newly spawned Christologies often ranked high in contextualization but seemingly lacked antiquity and consensus. Often these "heresies" pursued genuinely noble ends, such as constructing a theodicy while attempting an integration of Christian theism with platonic cosmogony (gnosticism), maintaining a high Christology in conjunction with a platonic disdain for the material world (docetism), safeguarding the oneness of God (modalism), or retaining the monarchy of the Father without completely disparaging the divine nature of the Son (subordinationism). The heresies were not trying to undermine belief in Christ; rather, they were trying to contextualize it, to explain its coherence anew, and to make it palatable in the existing cultural environment by utilizing the philosophical resources on hand. Yet these dissident Christologies were ultimately rejected by an emerging majority on different grounds: (1) they failed to commend themselves as built on apostolic foundations, (2) they seemingly lacked scriptural warrant, (3) they had questionable internal coherence, or (4) they espoused dubious consequences for everyday life. It was not that these views were suppressed by a group of bishops who insisted on imposing their own narrow dogma on diverse group who was self-consciously pluralistic and tolerated gnostic and kenotic Christologies side by side. Far more likely, the Jesus in the Apocalypse of Peter was discarded because he was not "according to the Scriptures." Docetism was thought dubious because it made a mockery of the cross and the Eucharist. Subordinationism was censured because it tore apart the fabric of the gospel and entailed that the worship of Jesus was blasphemous. Modalism was rejected on the grounds that it turned the baptism of Jesus into a ridiculous moment of divine ventriloquism. To give a specific example, Simon Gathercole asserts that the Gospel of Judas did not catch on because it presents a disembodied Jesus, a loveless Jesus, and a Jesus without suffering. The result was a Jesus whom many did not find attractive for veneration.[7]

7. Simon J. Gathercole, *The Gospel of Judas* (Oxford: Oxford University Press, 2007), 162–71.

Adoptionism

One of the most potent if not persistent heresies of the second and third centuries was adoptionism. The problem with adoptionism was that although Jesus's divine sonship was arguably the most characteristic of Christians, claims about him,[8] those advocating an adoptionist view of divine sonship were perceived to be reducing Jesus to a human figure who had acquired divine status by merit. Whereas the proto-orthodox church said that this sonship preceded the incarnation ("eternally begotten" in the language of the church fathers), others insisted that Jesus's sonship had a historical beginning at some point: at his birth, baptism, or resurrection. In adoptionism there was a time when Jesus was not the Son of God. Divine sonship is not something that Jesus had possessed for all time, but something he attained in the course of his life.

There were a variety of types of adoptionism.[9] Common to all versions are basically two things. The first said that divine sonship was not essential to Jesus. Rather, it was acquired at some point in his terrestrial life. The second claimed that divine sonship is not ontological but honorific. Thus, sonship is not derived from Jesus's unique filial relationship to Israel's God, but is conferred as a legal fiction even if it means elevation to divine status. Adoptionism is normally associated with (1) the Ebionites who are alleged to have been a Jewish Christian sect of the early to mid-second century; (2) Theodotus, a lay Christian and Roman cobbler of

8. The identification of Jesus as the "Son of God" or "God's Son" was widespread in early Christian preaching (Acts 9:20; 13:32–33; 2 Cor 1:9; Gal 1:16; 1 Thess 1:10), found in early confessional material (Rom 1:3–4), shaped readings of Scripture (Acts 13:33; Heb 1:5; 5:5; 2 Pet 1:17; Rev 12:5), and defined the whole matrix of fellowship and communion with God (Rom 8:29; 1 Cor 1:9; Gal 2:19–20; 4:6; Eph 4:13; Col 1:13).

9. According to John C. Cavadini, *The Last Christology of the West: Adoptionism in Spain and Gaul, 785–820* (Philadelphia: University of Philadelphia Press, 1993), 1: "'Adoptionism' is a word without a fixed historical reference, as there have been several theologies, historically unrelated, which have been given that name." For basic introductions to "adoptionism," I recommend J. N. D. Kelly, *Early Christian Doctrines*, 5th ed. (London: Continuum, 2001), 142–45; Justo L. González and Catherine Gunsalus González, *Heretics for Armchair Theologians* (Louisville: Westminster John Knox, 2008), 15–28; James L. Papandrea, *The Earliest Christologies: Five Images of Christ in the Postapostolic Age* (Downers Grove, IL: InterVarsity, 2016), 23–43.

the late second century and (3) Paul of Samosata, a bishop of Antioch in the third century who was deposed for his beliefs. Although adoptionism was rejected by the orthodox churches, this does not mean that all forms of adoptionism thereafter became extinct. Adoptionism has re-emerged from time to time, notably in Spain under Muslim suzerainty in the eighth century, and has found expression even in the modern period.[10]

A widespread assumption in modern scholarship is that the earliest recoverable Christology was adoptionism, and only later—with Paul, John, Ignatius of Antioch, and Justin Martyr—did an incarnational Christology fully develop, rise to dominate, and then attempt to dispel all competing accounts of Jesus's person.[11] Knox, an American scholar, contended that adoptionism corresponded more closely than any later belief with the actual experience of the early church, which knew Jesus to be a man declared to be Lord and Messiah. He put it bluntly: "That [Christology] began with 'adoptionism' and ended with 'incarnationism' is hardly open to doubt."[12] Dunn is similar, noting how the Ebionites held to an adoptionist Christology and yet that "heretical Jewish Christianity would appear to be not so very different from the faith of the first Jewish believers."[13] Bart Ehrman

---

10. The Spanish heresy is more properly called "Adoptianism," an idea that separated the divine Logos from the human Jesus so sharply that Jesus could only in an adoptive sense be God's Son. See Cavadini, *The Last Christology of the West*, and Cullen J. Chandler, "Heresy and Empire: The Role of the Adoptionist Controversy in Charlemagne's Conquest of the Spanish March," *IHR* 24 (2002): 505–27. In regard to modern adoptionists, see Wolfhart Pannenberg, *Jesus–God and Man* (Philadelphia: Westminster, 1968), 121.

11. Cf. Johannes Weiss, *Earliest Christianity: A History of the Period AD 30–150*, 2 vols. (New York: Harper, 1959) 1:118–33; Rudolf Bultmann, *Theology of the New Testament*, 2 vols. (London: SCM, 1952), 1:27, 50–52; Ernst Käsemann, "The Canon of the New Testament and the Unity of the Church," in *Essays on New Testament Themes*, SBT 41 (London: SCM, 1964), 215; Maurice Casey, *From Jewish Prophet to Gentile God: The Origins and Development of New Testament Christology* (Cambridge: James Clarke & Co., 1991), 106, 111–12.

12. John Knox, *The Church and the Reality of Christ* (London: Collins, 1963), 95; see further John Knox, *The Humanity and Divinity of Christ: A Study of Pattern in Christology* (Cambridge: Cambridge University Press, 1967), 5–8, 95–97.

13. Dunn, *Unity and Diversity in the New Testament*, 242; see further James D. G. Dunn, *Christology in the Making: A New Testament Inquiry into the Origins of the Doctrine of the Incarnation*, 2nd ed. (London: SCM, 1986), 33–36.

has suggested that if one of Jesus's followers had written a Gospel a year or so after his resurrection, one would find an "exaltation Christology," which described how Jesus "became the Son of God when God worked his greatest miracle on him, raising him from the dead and adopting him as his Son by exalting him to his right hand and bestowing upon him his very own power, prestige, and status."[14]

The Goal of This Book

My objective is to question this quasi-consensus that the earliest retrievable Christology was adoptionist. To that end, I intend to develop two central claims: (1) the first Christologies were hastily devised venerations of Jesus as a divine figure, which then crystallized over the next twenty years into a series of presentations of Jesus that were variations of a theme of incarnationalism, even if the details were still to be fully worked out; and (2) adoptionism originated as a particular second-century phenomenon driven largely by internal debates about preferred texts and socio-religious influences on reading them. So, when did Jesus get adopted as the Son of God? As we will see, probably in the second century, though precisely when will remain a matter of debate.

Given that objective, this study will proceed in several distinct stages. First, I will examine Rom 1:3–4 and materials in the Lucan speeches in Acts that are alleged to espouse a primitive adoptionist Christology whereby Jesus became the Son of God at his resurrection. Second, Mark's Gospel is purported to have been influenced by Greco-Roman accounts of the deification of human figures, which calls for an examination of deification in relation to the Jewish monotheism which shapes Mark's symbolic world. Third, it is often argued that several features of Mark's Gospel make it adoptionistic, not least the baptismal scene, and those features need to be weighed and tested in light of the Gospel as a whole. Fourth, there are several texts and groups from the second century alleged to have been adoptionist. The Shepherd of Hermas has a very eclectic and opaque

---

14. Bart D. Ehrman, *How Jesus Became God: The Exaltation of a Jewish Preacher from Galilee* (New York: HarperOne, 2014), 246.

Christology which is sometimes associated with adoptionism. Some scholars routinely claim that the Ebionites had an adoptionist Christology, so it is worth studying who this obscure group was and what they actually believed about Jesus. Closely following that I will examine the Theodotians—an incontestable adoptionist movement—and what their specific articulation of adoptionism tells us about the origins of adoptionist Christology. Fifth, and somewhat excursively, I will briefly survey and critique some recent manifestations of adoptionism in modern theology.

CHAPTER 2

Appointed the Son of God
by Resurrection from the Dead

Many scholars think that in the most primitive Christology, Jesus was thought to have been adopted by God at his resurrection. The earliest Christology, then, was that Jesus was a human figure who, on account of his faithful life, was exalted to divine status and "appointed" or "made" the Son of God by being raised from the dead. It is frequently argued that the creedal formula in Rom 1:3–4 and fragments from the evangelistic preaching in the Book of Acts demonstrate that this was in all probability the earliest view of Jesus circulating within the Jesus movement. To those texts we now turn.

The Son of God *in Power*: Rom 1:3–4

Ground zero in the debate about adoptionist Christology in the early church is the creedal-like formula we find in Rom 1:3–4. If Paul wrote his letter to the Romans from Cenchreae near Corinth around 55/56 CE and if this creedal formula is pre-Pauline, we have here an early testimony about Jesus's identity within some twenty years of his death.[1]

---

1. The creedal nature of the text is suggested grammatically by the substantive participles that interrupt christological titulature, the asyndetic construction, and the clear parallelism. The pre-Pauline nature of the text is implied by construal of the flesh-Spirit antithesis and the Semitic nature of "Spirit of holiness." In addition, the verb ὁρίζω ("I appoint") is a hapax legomenon in the Pauline corpus, and this is the only explicit ref-

11

εὐαγγέλιον θεοῦ	the gospel of God
ὃ προεπηγγείλατο διὰ τῶν	that he promised beforehand through
προφητῶν αὐτοῦ ἐν γραφαῖς ἁγίαις	his prophets in the Holy Scriptures

περὶ τοῦ υἱοῦ αὐτοῦ	regarding his Son,

τοῦ γενομένου	who was descended
ἐκ σπέρματος Δαυὶδ	from the seed of David,
κατὰ σάρκα,	according to the flesh

τοῦ ὁρισθέντος	who was appointed
υἱοῦ θεοῦ ἐν δυνάμει	the Son of God in power
κατὰ πνεῦμα ἁγιωσύνης ἐξ	by the Spirit of holiness from
ἀναστάσεως νεκρῶν,	resurrection of the dead:

Ἰησοῦ Χριστοῦ τοῦ κυρίου ἡμῶν	Jesus Christ our Lord.

An important caveat is required before we explore this passage. The creedal formulas and traditional materials that we find scattered across the New Testament[2] are intended as abbreviated confessions of faiths, succinct to a point but ultimately insufficient, functioning as symbols and signs of a wider body of beliefs. They are not comprehensive in their affirmations, and they make no denials. They are, in other words, the ancient equivalent

---

erence to Jesus's Davidic descent in the undisputed Pauline letters. See further Robert Jewett, "The Redaction and Use of an Early Christian Confession in Romans 1:3–4," in *The Living Text: Essays in Honor of Ernest W. Saunders*, ed. Dennis E. Groh and Robert Jewett (New York: University Press of America, 1985), 100–102. Alternatively, Vern S. Poythress, "Is Romans 1:3–4 a Pauline Confession after All?" *ExpTim* 87 [1976]: 180–83, thinks Paul uses traditional material in a free composition. James Scott, *Adoption as Sons of God*, WUNT 2.48 (Tübingen: Mohr Siebeck, 1992), 229–36, considers evidence for a pre-Pauline tradition "less impressive." Similar is Aquila H. I. Lee, *From Messiah to Preexistent Son* (Eugene, OR: Wipf & Stock, 2005), 263, and Christopher G. Whitsett, "Son of God, Seed of David: Paul's Messianic Exegesis on Romans [1]:3–4," *JBL* 119 (2000): 661–81. See Robert Matthew Calhoun, *Paul's Definition of the Gospel in Romans 1*, WUNT 2.316 (Tübingen: Mohr Siebeck, 2011), 92–106, for a point-by-point response to Jewett. Calhoun thinks Paul draws on traditional material, not quoting a text, but evoking a wealth of tradition.

2. See e.g., Rom 1:3–4; 4:25; Phil 2:5–11; Col 1:15–20; 1 Cor 15:3–7; 1 Tim 3:16; 1 Pet 3:18–19, 22.

of a doctrinal bumper sticker or the condensing of a complex theological topic into a single message. So we should not assume that these densely packed sentences were the totality of what people believed about Jesus, or that early Christians were disinterested or even opposed to anything else that might be said about Jesus. The early christological formulas in the New Testament do not reflect the remnants of independent Christologies but rather signal efforts to articulate convictions shared among various Christian groups.[3] A passage like Rom 1:3–4 makes a limited number of affirmations that can be pulled in one or more directions in regard to Jesus's pre-existence, earthly career, current status, future, and relationship to the Father.[4] We have no way of knowing whether such a statement precedes or presupposes other terse affirmations, such as God's sending of the pre-existent Jesus (Rom 8:3; Gal 4:4–5; Phil 2:6–8; 2 Cor 8:9), an atonement tradition (Rom 3:24–25; 1 Cor 5:6; Gal 3:13), the saving significance of his death and resurrection (Rom 4:25; 1 Thess 4:14; 1 Cor 15:3–5; 2 Cor 5:15), Jesus's exaltation to the Father's right hand (Rom 8:34; Phil 2:9–11; Eph 1:20), Jesus's return as judge (Rom 2:16; 14:10; 2 Cor 5:10; 1 Thess 1:10), and the profession of Jesus as "Lord" (Rom 10:9–13; 1 Cor 8:6; 12:3; 16:22; Phil 2:9–11). In other words, no scholar can truly say with confidence: This is what they *first* believed, and this is *all* that they believed!

Paul inserts this creedal material into his opening prescript to create an immediate rapport with the Roman believers—most of whom he does not know directly—in order to showcase his apostolic credentials and the fact that they share a common faith as reflected in this creedal summary. The accent on the creed falls squarely on the identity of Jesus as the divine "Son," born of Davidic descent, installed as the "Son of God in power" by virtue of being raised from the dead, and who is further acclaimed as "our Lord." Paul's gospel centers upon the christologically dense declaration that Jesus is the Messiah, Israel's long-waited deliverer, that his resurrection has inaugurated the beginning of the end of the ages, and that he possesses superlative status as "Lord."[5] When Rom 1:3–4 is taken with Rom 15:8–9, 12, Paul is effectively bookending Romans with Jesus's

3. Petr Pokorný, *The Genesis of Christology* (Edinburgh: T&T Clark, 1987), 105.
4. See similarly Dunn, *Christology in the Making*, 62–63.
5. Michael F. Bird, *Romans*, The Story of God Bible Commentary (Grand Rapids: Zondervan, 2016), 21–24.

messianic identity, so that: "Christ's Davidic heritage fulfils the promises and confirms God's faithfulness to the Jews; his appointment—that is, his resurrection—relates him to the Gentiles as the mode of their inclusion in the family of Abraham and the rule of the Messiah."[6]

Delving deeper into Rom 1:3–4, the creedal formula has been said to imply an adoptionist or exaltation Christology whereby Jesus—a descendant of David—is invested with divine sonship at his resurrection. According to Walter Schmithals, "The oldest and classical testimony to adoption Christology is found in Rom. 1:3–4" where "Jesus is presented only as one of many descendants of David, and such a lineage is a necessary presupposition for his adoption and exaltation as the messianic Son of God."[7] For Ehrman, "From this creed one can see that Jesus is not simply the human messiah, and he is not simply the Son of Almighty God. He is both things, in two phases: first he is the Davidic Messiah predicted in Scripture, and second he is the exalted divine Son." Ehrman thinks that Paul might have wanted to embellish this description further since his own view of Jesus included pre-existence, yet for the original framer of the creed, "Jesus was the messiah from the house of David during his earthly life, but at the resurrection he was made something much more than that. The resurrection was Jesus's exaltation into divinity."[8] Even Gordon Fee concedes that "if this were the only text of its kind in the [Pauline] corpus, one could easily settle for an adoptionist Christology—Jesus becomes the 'eternal' Son at his resurrection and subsequent exaltation."[9]

A number of factors can be said to support this interpretation. First, a transition of status is envisaged as Jesus seemingly goes from an earthly position as a Son of David to a divine state as the Son of God by way of resurrection. Second, the verb ὁρίζω means "to appoint, designate, declare" and we might just as well translate it as "install."[10] In which case, Jesus is not just "publicly identified" (CEB) as the Son of God, but is concretely

---

6. Whitsett, "Son of God, Seed of David," 677.

7. Walter Schmithals, *The Theology of the First Christians*, trans. O. C. Dean Jr. (Louisville: Westminster: John Knox, 1997), 89–90.

8. Ehrman, *How Jesus Became God*, 221–22.

9. Gordon D. Fee, *Pauline Christology: An Exegetical-Theological Study* (Peabody, MA: Hendrickson, 2007), 544.

10. BDAG, 723.

made the Son of God by divine fiat after the divine act of raising him from the dead. Third, the prepositional phrase ἐν δυνάμει ("in power") is thought by many to be a Pauline addition to the creed, so that Paul wants Jesus to be designated as the Son-of-God-in-power, whereas the original creed was content with Jesus becoming the Son of God without further elaboration. Fourth, the resurrection is what marks the beginning of Jesus's divine sonship, regardless of whether the preposition ἐκ in ἐξ ἀναστάσεως νεκρῶν ("from/since/by resurrection from the dead") signals origin ("from resurrection"), temporal relationship ("since resurrection"), or even means ("by" or "on the grounds of resurrection").

Those arguments, however, are by no means definitive and we have good grounds for questioning them. As we will see, it is not at all certain that this creed imagines Jesus becoming a/the Son of God at his resurrection. We could have here a transition from one state of divine sonship to another state of divine sonship.[11]

First, we have to remember that the titles "Son of David" and "Son of God" were both designations for Israel's "Messiah." That is rooted in the Old Testament where we find the promise that one of David's descendants will be God's own son (2 Sam 7:10–14; Pss 89:4, 26, 35–37; 132:11–12, 17–18), which is why Israel's king was ritually celebrated as a divine son (Pss 2:7; 72:1), and why the prophets looked forward to a Davidic descendent to deliver the nation (Isa 11, Jer 23; Ezek 34, 37; Mic 5). We find similar phenomenon in Jewish intertestamental literature that looks forward to the coming of an eschatological Son of David, the Messiah, who is sometimes called the "Son of God" (Pss. Sol. 17.4, 21; 4Q174 3.7–13; 4Q246 2.1–3; 4Q369 frg. 1, 2.6–7)[12] and the New Testament likewise puts Son of David in

---

11. This is why Dunn, *Christology in the Making*, 3, hedges his bets: "What is clear, on either alternative, is that *the resurrection of Jesus was regarded as of central significance in determining his divine sonship*, either as his installation to a status and prerogatives not enjoyed before, or as a major enhancement of a sonship already enjoyed" (italics original). Later, James D. G. Dunn, *Beginning from Jerusalem*, vol. 2 of *Christianity in the Making* (Grand Rapids: Eerdmans, 2009), 217, ceases hedging and clearly affirms the later view: "For him at least [i.e., Paul], the resurrection marked an enhanced, not an initial bestowal, of Jesus' sonship—'Son of God *in power*'" (italics original).

12. This demolishes the claim of Wilhelm Bousset, *Kyrios Christos: A History of the Belief in Christ from the Beginnings of Christianity to Irenaeus*, trans. John E. Steely

close proximity to Son of God (Mark 12:35–37; Luke 1:32).[13] In the context of Rom 1:3–4, Paul's description of Jesus as "from the seed of David" marks him out as the royal-eschatological Davidic deliverer, the Son of David. Just like the title "Root of Jesse" (Isa 11:10; Rom 15:12), this description is meant to elicit the prophetic promise of a coming Davidic descendent, a new Davidic king, who is otherwise known as the "Messiah," and who is elsewhere called "Son of God." Thus, if the Seed/Son of David *is* the messianic Son of God, then we cannot say that divine sonship begins at a later point like resurrection.[14] That is because, in the creed we are examining, divine sonship is already embedded in the designation of Jesus as the Davidic descendent prior to his resurrection. By itself, that suggests that Jesus's resurrection transforms his status from *one type* of divine sonship (Davidic) to *another type* of divine sonship (in power). The resurrection is a declarative, quasi-forensic vindication of Jesus's messianic sonship. However, it is more than that, since the resurrection enhances or upgrades Jesus's divine sonship into a new mode of expression where he shares more fully in divine executive power and majesty.[15] The parallelism between v. 3 and v. 4 is not antithetical, but marks a narratival progression as God's Son shifts from exercising his messianic mission in human weakness to using

---

(Waco, TX: Baylor University Press, 2013), 206–10, that the title "Son of God" did not derive from Jewish messianism and primitive Palestinian Christianity.

13. On Jewish messianic expectations, see Michael F. Bird, *Are You the One Who Is to Come? The Historical Jesus and the Messianic Question* (Grand Rapids: Baker, 2007), 31–62.

14. While "Son of David" and "Son of God" both imply the status of *messias designatus*, the New Testament expands the meaning of "Son of God" in at least two senses: (1) It reflects Jesus's own consciousness of his unique filial relationship with Israel's God, whom he regarded as his Father (Mark 12:6; 13:32; 14:36; Matt 6:9; Matt 11:27/Luke 10:22; shaping Christian prayer in Rom 8:16 and Gal 4:6); and (2) Divine sonship is sometimes used to express Jesus's pre-existent state as the Father sends his Son into the world (John 3:16–17; 5:23; 10:36; Rom 8:3; Gal 4:4–5; 1 John 4:9–10, 14; Col 1:15).

15. James D. G. Dunn, *Romans*, WBC, 2 vols. (Dallas, TX: Word, 1988), 1:14; Maurice Casey, *From Jewish Prophet to Gentile God: The Origins and Development of New Testament Christology* (Cambridge: James Clarke & Co., 1991), 111; Martin Hengel, *Studies in Early Christology* (Edinburgh: T&T Clark, 1995), 11; Craig Blomberg, *From Pentecost to Patmos: Acts to Revelation, An Introduction and Survey* (Nottingham: Apollos, 2006), 237.

his newly acquired divine prerogatives of power in his post-resurrection state.[16]

Second, the assumption that Paul himself added ἐν δυνάμει ("in power") to the creed in order to mitigate its adoptionist content is dubious.[17]

For a start, we simply do not know if Paul added or subtracted anything from the creed; he may well just have transmitted it as he himself had received it (on Paul passing on "traditions" see 1 Cor 11:2, 23, 15:1–3, 2 Thess 2:15, 3:6). Even if the creed is an amalgam of prior sources and editors ahead of Paul's own cosmetic redaction, it is almost futile to try to establish the composition history, just as it is futile to try and figure out the order that a jigsaw puzzle was put together. Indeed, the attempt of some scholars to detect three distinct stages of development in the creed from an original Jewish Christian provenance, to a Hellenistic Christian setting, and then to Paul's own editing, is simply fanciful.[18] Furthermore, the old assumption of a "Jewish Christianity" that was insulated from a later "Hellenistic Christianity" has been universally abandoned because of the now widely held view that all of first-century Judaism had been influenced by Hellenism to some degree and that Greek-speakers were part of the church from its very beginning. With the demise of the Jewish/Greek dichotomy goes also the assumption that early Christology must have evolved from an early adoptionist Christology while in Jewish Christianity to Christologies of pre-existence and incarnation when transported

16. See similarly Paul Beasley-Murray, "Romans 1:3f: An Early Confession of Faith in the Lordship of Jesus," *TynBul* 31 (1980): 152.

17. See Simon J. Gathercole, "What Did the First Christians Think about Jesus?" in *How God Became Jesus: The Real Origins of Belief in Jesus' Divine Nature*, ed. Michael F. Bird (Grand Rapids: Zondervan, 2014), 105–6. Dunn, *Romans*, 1:6, suggests that the reasons for treating ἐν δυνάμει as an insertion rest on an older view that the Davidic Messiah could not be thought of as God's Son, with the result that "Son of David" could not stand in parallel to "Son of God," but such an objection is overthrown by the discovery of the Dead Sea Scrolls (esp. 4Q174) that show that the Davidic Messiah could be regarded as God's Son.

18. See e.g., Heinrich Schlier, "Zu Röm 1.3f," in *Neues Testament und Geschichte, Historisches Geschehen und Deutung im Neuen Testament. Oscar Cullmann zum 70. Geburtstag*, ed. Heinrich Baltensweiler and Bo Reicke (Zürich: Theologischer Verlag, 1972), 207–18, and Jewett, "Redaction," 100–102. Note also the critique of that view in Matthew W. Bates, "A Christology of Incarnation and Enthronement: Romans 1:3–4 as Unified, Nonadoptionist, and Nonciliatory," *CBQ* 77 (2015): 110–25.

JESUS THE ETERNAL SON

to a Hellenistic setting.[19] That evolutionary scheme flounders because it can be turned on its head with Jewish sources describing a pre-existent and heavenly figure like "the Son of Man" in the Similitudes of 1 Enoch[20] and Greco-Roman sources envisaging emperors becoming deified upon death and their designated heirs thereafter adopted to divine sonship. So, contrary to received scholarly wisdom, one could easily envisage a scenario where pre-existence and incarnation appear first in a Jewish setting and only later does adoptionism come onto the scene when Christianity moved into a Roman setting! In brief, we have no way of knowing what Paul added to or subtracted from the creed; to say otherwise is to engage in self-delusion. Plus the proposed evolutionary scheme in which editing of the creed took place, depicting a Jewish Christianity with its adoptionism and a later Hellenistic Christianity with its Christologies of pre-existence and incarnation, flounders because it postulates dichotomies (Judaism vs. Hellenism) and developments (adoptionism first and pre-existence later) that simply do not exist as far as our sources are concerned.

Furthermore, if the original form of the creed was discordant with Paul's own Christology of pre-existence, then we hasten to wonder why he used it at all, particularly when his aim in writing was to win the Romans over to his particular expression of the gospel. It is counter-intuitive for Paul to cite this creed as evidence of the common faith that he shared with his readers and then to amend it because it was christologically inadequate.[21] Paul does not expand an adoptionist creed to include pre-existence as much as he uses the creed to explain what he means by "his Son" in v. 3, and he evidently found it congenial to his own christological convictions that included pre-existence, incarnation, and exaltation.[22] Viewed that way, we can see a clear progression in Rom 1:3–4: the one who was, in Paul's view, already "his Son" (v. 3a),[23] becomes the Son of

19. See I. Howard Marshall, *The Origins of New Testament Christology* (England: InterVarsity, 1977), 32–42.

20. See 1 En. 48.3, 6; 62.7.

21. Dunn, *Romans*, 1:14.

22. Scott, *Adoption as Sons of God*, 234–35, followed by Lee, *Messiah to Preexistent Son*, 265.

23. C. E. B. Cranfield, *The Epistle to the Romans*, 2 vols., ICC (Edinburgh: T & T Clark, 1975–1979), 1:58, rightly observes that the position of "his son" at the head of the

David by a human birth and thus enters into fleshly existence (v. 3b),[24] and is then divinely appointed to be the glorious Son of God in power upon his resurrection (v. 4).[25] Paul's implicit narrative remains true to his understanding of the kerygma and betrays no hesitancies that this creed is a Trojan horse smuggling in something less than appropriate for spelling out Jesus's person and identity.[26]

Finally, the presumption of a Pauline addition here is rather convenient because the current form of the creed with the words ἐν δυνάμει portrays Jesus not as becoming the Son of God for the first time, but becoming the Son of God in a new way, in power. Precisely because the phrase ἐν δυνάμει is injurious to the thesis that the creed espouses an early adoptionist Christology, it becomes necessary to find a way to erase it.[27] Ehrman contends that the original form of the creed was adoptionistic, so "Paul may have wanted to add this phrase ["in power"] because according to his own theology, Jesus was the Son of God before the resurrection, but he

---

confession controls both the participle clauses in v. 3 and v. 4 and implies "that the One who was born of the seed of David was already Son of God before, and independently of, the action denoted by the second participle." Similar is Oscar Cullmann, *The Christology of the New Testament* (Philadelphia: Westminster, 1959), 292, who writes: "Jesus is the 'Son of God' from the beginning. At least this appears to be Paul's understanding when in v. 3 he makes 'Son' the subject of the two-part confession. But since the resurrection, the eternal divine sonship manifests itself ἐν δυνάμει; the Son of God becomes the *Kyrios*." Fee, *Pauline Christology*, 544, detects a point "where Davidic Son and eternal Son merge." See also Matthew W. Bates, *The Birth of the Trinity: Jesus, God, and the Spirit in New Testament and Early Christian Interpretations of the Old Testament* (Oxford: Oxford University Press, 2015), 158–60, and Bates, "Christology of Incarnation and Enthronement," 115–16.

24. A point that accords with Paul's thought elsewhere where Jesus takes on human flesh (Rom 8:3), human form (Phil 2:7), and a human birth (Gal 4:4).

25. Lee, *Messiah to Preexistent Son*, 269.

26. Against Adela Y. Collins and John J. Collins, *King as Messiah and Son of God: Divine, Human, and Angelic Messianic Figures in Biblical and Related Literature* (Grand Rapids: Eerdmans, 2008), 117–18, 209, we need not regard a Christology of pre-existence in Rom 1:3–4 as an alternative to a Christology where the messiah, as Son of God, is elevated to the status of being "in power."

27. Bates, "A Christology of Incarnation and Enthronement," 124, says that "this rationale assumes what it is trying to prove, because there is no good reason to posit that the original protocreed lacked ἐν δυνάμει, nor is there any real evidence in favour of an original adoptionist Christology here apart from the redactional hypothesis itself."

was exalted to an even higher state at the resurrection."[28] I see no reason for regarding ἐν δυνάμει as a Pauline addition. The corollary is that the creed here identifies Jesus as exalted to a higher state of divine sonship beyond what he previously possessed. The likely meaning of "Son of God in power" is that Jesus is installed to a new position of divine lordship and life-giving power.[29]

Third, it is implausible that the early creed envisaged Jesus becoming a divine being upon his resurrection.[30] For a start, in the Jewish world "Son of God" does not mean a human person who has lived a meritorious life and received divine sonship after bodily resurrection as a reward for his herculean labors. Israel was God's son by virtue of election (Exod 4:22; Hos 11:1), Israel's kings were acclaimed as divine sons upon their enthronement (Ps 2:7), and angels held a type of divine sonship because of their heavenly nature (Gen 6:2–4; Deut 32:8; Job 1:6–12; Pss 29:1; 89:6). Biblical figures like Enoch (Gen 5:24; Heb 11:25) and Elijah (2 Kgs 2:11) were thought to have been assumed into heaven. They became immortal but never in the tradition were they thereafter called Sons of God.[31] Lazarus was raised from the dead in the Gospel of John (John 11:44) and so where the two witnesses in the Book of Revelation (11:11–12). This act did not indicate that they had attained divine status or were granted divine sonship. Certainly, there are Greco-Roman traditions of Greek heroes and Roman emperors becoming divine after death

28. Ehrman, *How Jesus Became God*, 224.

29. On how this relates to the rest of Romans, Joshua Jipp, *Christ is King: Paul's Royal Ideology* (Minneapolis: Fortress, 2015), 177, insightfully comments: "Thus the resurrected-enthroned Son of God's existence is now marked by the qualities and attributes of the Spirit, foremost . . . are the power to bring the eschatological life associated with resurrection (Rom. 8:9–11), familial relation to God (8:14–17), and liberation from hostile lords that allows for the ability to please and worship God (7:5–6; 8:5–8)."

30. Similarly, it is unlikely that Jesus was designated as Messiah on the basis of his resurrection, since resurrection never necessitated or implied messianic status. See Bird, *Are You the One Who Is to Come?*, 64–66, and similarly Dunn, *Beginning from Jerusalem*, 91, 217.

31. The only near-exception I have found is T. Ab. Rec. A 12.4–5, in which the patriarch Abel is described in a glorified state as "like a son of God," which is tantamount to being "equal to the angels" (Luke 20:36; Ascen. Isa. 9.9; Philo, *Sacr.* 5; Sir 45.2). There is no connotation here of messianic status, divine prerogatives, or sharing in God's reign.

through apotheosis or deification, but there is one big difference. Upon death the emperor became a *divus* (deified one), whereas it was the emperor's designated heir left on earth who was then called *divi filius* ("son of the divine one"). We know of no one from antiquity who became a Son of God by resurrection.[32]

A more likely scenario is that while the resurrection did not mark the beginning of Jesus's divine sonship, it instead signified a change in the ages with a consequent change in the mode and function of divine sonship for Jesus.[33] The ἀναστάσεως νεκρῶν (literally "resurrection of the dead ones") is a generalizing plural, and there is no pronoun "his," inserted by some English translations. So it is not directly about Jesus's own resurrection, but refers more properly to the general resurrection of the dead on the last day, of which Jesus's own resurrection to be sure can be considered the beginning or the first-fruits (1 Cor 15:23). Therefore, because Jesus is the "firstborn from the dead" (Col 1:18; Rev 1:5; cf. Rom 8:29), he enters into a new mode of divine sonship as the first of the "sons of the resurrection." His humanity is now immortal and glorified, "equal to the angels" as Luke calls it (Luke 20:35). It is in this transformed state of divine sonship that he now exercises new regal and priestly functions, which Paul spells out later in Romans as interceding, ruling, and judging (Rom 2:16; 8:34; 14:9–10; cf. 1 Cor 15:25 and Heb 2:9). Paul says later as well that believers already have been adopted to divine sonship by virtue of the Spirit's indwelling (Rom

32. On the Roman emperor as "Son of God," see Winter, *Divine Honours for the Caesars*, 67–71.

33. Somewhat similar is Paula Fredriksen, *From Jesus to Christ: The Origins of the New Testament Images of Jesus* (New Haven, CT: Yale University Press, 1988), 141, and J. R. Daniel Kirk, *Unlocking Romans: Resurrection and the Justification of God* (Grand Rapids: Eerdmans, 2008), 40–41. Here I depart from N. T. Wright, *Paul and the Faithfulness of God*, vol. 4 of *Christian Origins and the Question of God* (London: SPCK, 2014), 700, who thinks resurrection here "unveils what was there before, it does not confer or create a new status or identity for Jesus. The key word *horisthentos*, with its root meaning to do with 'marking a boundary,' and hence 'defining' or 'determining,' has to do with the public clarification, validation or vindication of a previously made claim, not with a claim or status newly introduced." In my thinking, there is a change, an eschatological escalation not in the fact of divine sonship, but how that sonship is displayed and discharged. Similar is Fee, *Pauline Christology*, 544, who thinks "Rom 1:4 should be understood as the Father's and Spirit's vindication of the eternal Son."

JESUS THE ETERNAL SON

8:15–17; cf. Gal 4:5) and yet they await a future adoption to eschatological sonship with the redemption of their bodies. That will happen when the Spirit raises them up at the last day and they are glorified with Christ and conformed to the image of the Son (Rom 8:11, 15–18, 23, 29–30).[34] So just as Rom 1:4 declared that the Holy Spirit is the means by which the Messiah is appointed as the Son of God in power at the resurrection, so also the Spirit is the instrument for the adoption of believers as sons of God at the resurrection in Rom 8.[35] In effect, Paul's purpose in Rom 1:4 is to "foreshadow the manner in which Christ's sonship is the prototype for the rest of humanity."[36]

Fourth, the reception history of Rom 1:3–4 shows a distinct lack of interest in pro-adoptionist readings. The text was used to elaborate upon Jesus's human and divine natures.[37] For example, Ignatius of Antioch, when discussing the mystery of the cross, alludes to Rom 1:3–4 by referring to "Jesus the Christ, [who] was conceived by Mary according to God's plan, both from the seed of David and of the Holy Spirit," and shortly after he praises his readers for their unity "in one faith and one Jesus Christ, who physically was a descendent of David, who is Son of Man and Son of God."[38] Ignatius opens another letter with stress on Jesus's two natures as "he is truly of the family of David with respect to human descent, Son of God with respect to divine will and power."[39] Joshua Jipp maps a similar pattern of reading Rom 1:3–4 focused on

34. See further Scott, *Adoption as Sons of God*, 221–66 (esp. 222–23, 244–45, 256).

35. Scott, *Adoption as Sons of God*, 256. Jipp, *Christ Is King*, 118–19, adds, "The messianic king is the first one to experience resurrection, but his enthronement secures the certainty that his offspring will follow his path."

36. Joshua W. Jipp, "Ancient, Modern, and Future Interpretations of Romans 1:3–4: Reception History and Biblical Interpretation," *JTI* 3 (2009): 237, and similarly Scott, *Adopted as Sons of God*, 244–45: "Rom. 1:4 implies that the Son's resurrection is prototypical of the future resurrection of the dead (ἀνάστασις νεκρῶν). Rom. 8 goes beyond this by arguing that those who are in Christ will participate in the resurrection and sonship of the Son by being adopted as sons of God at a Spirit-mediated resurrection. The correlation of Rom. 8 with Rom. 1:4 is thus complete and unmistakable: believers will share in the destiny of him who was 'appointed Son of God in power by the Holy Spirit at the resurrection of the dead.'"

37. Jipp, "Ancient, Modern, and Future Interpretations of Romans 1:3–4."

38. Ignatius, *Eph.* 18.2; 20.2 (Holmes).

39. Ignatius, *Smyr* 1.1 (Holmes).

Jesus's human and divine natures in Tertullian, Irenaeus, Origen, John Chrysostom, Theodoret of Cyrus, Athanasius of Alexandria, Cyril of Alexandria, and Apollinaris of Laodicea. While several of these authors are aware of the possibility of adoptionist readings of Rom 1:4—notably Origen, Chrysostom, and Theodoret, they do not regard them as particularly persuasive paradigms for reading the text. Jipp also counsels that before rejecting these readings as merely dogmatic impositions, one should note how they exhibit a remarkable degree of coherence with the internal argument of Paul's letter that shows a concern for Jesus's fleshly existence (Rom 8:3), Jesus's appointment to sonship as a parallel to believers' adoption to divine sonship (Rom 8:29), and the stress on Jesus's Davidic identity (Rom 15:7–12). As John of Damascus wrote, "He who is by nature Son of God became first-born amongst us who were made by adoption and grace sons of God, and stand to Him in the relation of brothers."[40] If presented with a choice of reading Rom 1:3–4 *either* as part of a hypothetical reconstruction of the evolution of Christology from Palestinian to Hellenistic *or* reading Rom 1:3–4 as part of Paul's unfolding set of claims about Jesus's person and work across the letter, *then*, the patristic reading is perhaps more attractive than ordinarily supposed.

To sum up, according to Rom 1:3–4, the resurrection marks a transition from Jesus's messianic mode and earthly abode of divine sonship, to a new display of divine sonship defined by a regal function exercised from his heavenly position as God's vice-regent. Jesus the Son of David is raised up by the Spirit and so becomes the first son of the resurrection, arrayed in glorious immortality combined with heavenly royalty, the true meaning of "Son of God in power." By entering into this state Jesus thereafter makes it possible for his followers to be fully and finally incorporated into his own sonship at the general resurrection. To be even more concise about it, Jesus's divine sonship is transposed rather than triggered by resurrection, as he transitions from a Davidic Son of God to the Son of God in power who reigns on the Father's behalf and intercedes for his followers. There is indeed an adoption to divine sonship at the resurrection, but as Romans 8 makes clear, this is for believers who transfer from a spiritual

---

40. John of Damascus, *Orth. Faith.* 4.8 (Salmond, NPNF²).

sonship to an eschatological sonship. On this premise, early interpreters of Rom 1:3–4 found helpful material for affirming Jesus's human and divine natures and positing a link between Jesus's divine sonship and the adoption of believers.

This Jesus Made Lord and Messiah: Acts 2:36 (and 5:31, 13:33)

A second cohort of texts that has caused a groundswell of debate about early Christology and adoptionism consists of the speeches in Acts, not the least being Peter's Pentecost speech in Acts 2, which concludes with the words (2:36):

ἀσφαλῶς οὖν γινωσκέτω πᾶς οἶκος Ἰσραὴλ ὅτι καὶ κύριον αὐτὸν καὶ χριστὸν ἐποίησεν ὁ θεός, τοῦτον τὸν Ἰησοῦν ὃν ὑμεῖς ἐσταυρώσατε	Therefore, let the entire house of Israel know most assuredly that God has made him both Lord and Messiah, this Jesus whom you crucified.

John Knox asked, "[H]ow can this passage be interpreted to mean anything else than that the man Jesus, crucified simply as such, was at the resurrection exalted to his present messianic status?"[41] After all, in context the passage says that God "made" (ἐποίησεν) the crucified and risen Jesus (see Acts 2:32–34) into "Lord and Messiah" after God raised him from the dead. Ulrich Wilckens could speak of the passage as a *locus classicus* for an old primitive adoptionistic Christology.[42] What is more, such adoptionism appears congruent with several other Lucan speeches that express the same conviction that Jesus's messiahship, sonship, and lordship was attained upon his resurrection and ascension:

---

41. Knox, *Humanity and Divinity*, 8. See similarly C. K. Barrett, *A Critical and Exegetical Commentary on the Acts of the Apostles*, 2 vols., ICC (Edinburgh: T&T Clark, 1994), 1:140–41, 151–52.

42. Ulrich Wilckens, *Missionsreden der Apostelgeschichte: Form- und Traditionsgeschichtliche Untersuchungen*, 3rd ed., WMANT 5 (Zürich: Neurkirchenener Verlag, 1974), 171 ("Der Satz 2 36 wird vielfach von den Exegeten als alte, vorlukanische Formel und darin geradezu als locus classicus für ein alte primitive, 'adoptianische' Christologie in Anspruch genommen").

Acts 5:31 Peter's speech before the Sanhedrin in Jerusalem

ὁ θεὸς τῶν πατέρων ἡμῶν ἤγειρεν Ἰησοῦν ὃν ὑμεῖς διεχειρίσασθε κρεμάσαντες ἐπὶ ξύλου· τοῦτον ὁ θεὸς ἀρχηγὸν καὶ σωτῆρα ὕψωσεν τῇ δεξιᾷ αὐτοῦ [τοῦ] δοῦναι μετάνοιαν τῷ Ἰσραὴλ καὶ ἄφεσιν ἁμαρτιῶν.

The God of our ancestors raised Jesus—whom you killed by hanging him on a tree. Yet God exalted him to his own right hand as Prince and Savior that he might extend repentance to Israel and the forgiveness of sins.

Acts 13:32–33 Paul's synagogue speech in Pisidian Antioch

Καὶ ἡμεῖς ὑμᾶς εὐαγγελιζόμεθα τὴν πρὸς τοὺς πατέρας ἐπαγγελίαν γενομένην, ὅτι ταύτην ὁ θεὸς ἐκπεπλήρωκεν τοῖς τέκνοις [αὐτῶν] ἡμῖν ἀναστήσας Ἰησοῦν ὡς καὶ ἐν τῷ ψαλμῷ γέγραπται τῷ δευτέρῳ· υἱός μου εἶ σύ, ἐγὼ σήμερον γεγέννηκά σε.

We have come here to declare to you the good news that the promise made to our ancestors has come true. God has fulfilled it to their children by raising Jesus from the dead. As it says in the second psalm: "You are my son: today I have fathered you" [Ps 2:7].

The Lucan speeches exhibit a certain degree of homogeneity, conformed as they are to Luke's own theological and rhetorical interests that develop across Luke–Acts. Luke portrays Jesus as the Son of God from the moment of his conception (Luke 1:32, 35); nonetheless, several scholars believe that Luke has incorporated sources that are stamped with clear signs of an early adoptionist Christology, particularly given the citation of Ps 2:7 in Acts 13:33. Ehrman, commenting on Acts 2:36, writes: "The earliest followers of Jesus believed that the resurrection showed that God had exalted him to a position of grandeur and power. This verse is one piece of evidence. Here, in a preliterary tradition, we learn that it was precisely by raising Jesus from the dead that God had made him messiah and Lord."[43] Dunn shares a similar sentiment. On the basis of Rom 1:3–4 and portions of the Lucan speeches like Acts 2:36 and 13:33, he avers that "primitive Christian preaching seems to have regarded Jesus's resurrection as the day of his ap-

43. Ehrman, *How Jesus Became God*, 227–28.

pointment to divine sonship, as the events by which he became God's son." Dunn thinks we should be circumspect on whether the primitive church regarded Jesus as God's Son during his earthly ministry, but even if they recalled his intimate way of addressing God as *abba*, "they nevertheless regarded Jesus's resurrection as introducing him into a relationship with God decisively new, eschatologically distinct, and perhaps we should even say qualitatively different from what he had enjoyed before."[44] Dunn's postulation of an early adoptionism is suitably qualified and I think he moves in the right direction, but even then, I am not convinced that he and others are reading the evidence properly.

At the level of Luke's theology as a whole, that is, across all of Luke–Acts, it is difficult to imagine that Luke himself is expressing adoptionist views by clumsy insertions of adoptionistic sources. In the Lucan scheme, Jesus becomes *messias designatus* at his baptism (Luke 3:21), Jesus outs himself as a *messias petens* upon Peter's confession (Luke 9:20) and again at his trial (Luke 22:66–71), and Jesus becomes *messianicum regem* at his exaltation (Acts 2:36). What is paramount, at least in Luke's opinion, is that Jesus has always been "the Messiah, the Lord" (Luke 2:11).

In the specific case of Acts 2:36, the wider context and dense intertextuality of Peter's Pentecost sermon mitigates against an adoptionist reading. First, the citation of Joel 2:23–32 at Acts 2:17–21 climaxes with the refrain "everyone who calls on the name of the Lord will be saved." The "name" that saves is obviously Jesus (Acts 2.38; 3:6, 16; 4:10, 18, 30; 8:12, 16; 10:48; 19:5). Here we have a LXX κύριος text that, much like Paul in Rom 10:13, uses Joel 2:32 to identify Jesus with Israel's κύριος. Second, mention of Jesus's "mighty and wonderful deeds" (Acts 2:22) harks back to the exorcism stories where the demons acclaim Jesus as the "Son of God" who could destroy them (Luke 4:41; 8:28). While Jesus might be a "man accredited by God . . . by miracles, wonders, and signs," these mighty acts, specifically the exorcisms, are used in the Lucan story to point to his divine sonship. Third, Jesus's person and career were foreordained in God's eternal purposes, providing at a bare minimum an ideal form of pre-existence (Acts 2:23). Fourth, the citation of Ps 16:8–11 (Acts 2:25–32) makes Jesus paradoxically both the object of the psalm (in a prophetic sense) and also

44. Dunn, *Christology in the Making*, 38.

the subject of the psalm as its speaker (in a prosopological sense). According to Bates, Luke writes to the effect that "David, foreseeing these things, is speaking as a prophet in the prosopon of the Davidic messiah, the fruit of his own loins. And through David it is this Christ, the Son, who in turn is speaking about his own *future* resurrection."[45] This is not merely ideal pre-existence, but the prophetic and prosological pre-existence of Jesus as one who already speaks in Scripture. Fifth, the description of Jesus as the dispenser of the Spirit (Acts 2:33) is treated as proof of his exalted status. Not only that, but such a function tacitly suggests a divine identity for Jesus, because nowhere in the Old Testament or in Second Temple literature is anyone other than God described as the giver of the Spirit.[46] Sixth, the citation of Ps 110:1 (Acts 2:34–35) portrays Jesus rather than David as one who ascended to a position of heavenly enthronement and is identified as κύριος. Jesus is neither an angelomorphic being nor an exalted patriarch. Rather, he is a heavenly king who has been enthroned above all other beings, including David, and he reigns at God's right hand.[47] All in all, Peter's Pentecost sermon in Acts 2 seems to undermine rather than affirm any adoptionist Christology.[48] Because Jesus is identified with Israel's "Lord," he has a clear pre-history in God's purposes. His voice can already be heard in Scripture. Jesus is someone whom the reader knows to be the miracle-working Son of God; death is powerless to contain him, he is the dispenser of the Spirit, and Israel's exalted king. These connections show that Acts 2:36 should not be unhinged from its narrative moorings nor separated from the rest of the speech as if Luke has inadvertently included a fragment of an early adoptionist Christology that clearly conflicts with his own views.[49]

In addition, Jewish schemes of exaltation are not tantamount to

45. Bates, *Birth of the Trinity*, 154 (italics original).
46. Crispin Fletcher-Louis, *Luke-Acts: Angels, Christology, and Soteriology*, WUNT 2.94 (Tübingen: Mohr Siebeck, 1997), 22.
47. Eskola, *Messiah and the Throne*, 173.
48. Eskola, *Messiah and the Throne*, 176.
49. Contra e.g., Barrett, *Acts*, 1:151. Note esp. the comments of Robert Tannehill, *The Narrative Unity of Luke–Acts: A Literary Interpretation*, 2 vols. (Minneapolis: Fortress, 1986–90), 2:38: "The connections indicated show that Acts 2:36 should not be separated from the rest of the speech as a fragment of an early adoptionist Christology that conflicts with the narrator's views."

Greco-Roman notions of deification, and God's "making" him messiah and Lord need not involve an ontological change.[50] More likely, what transpires in Acts 2:36 with mention of how "God made him" (ἐποίησεν ὁ θεός) the Lord and Messiah is an expression of Luke's leitmotif of status reversal where God's word vindicates and empowers both Jesus and his people. Martin Hengel detects here not an adoptionist Christology "but a radical volte-face of the 'powers that be': God made him who had been delivered up by the leaders of the people for crucifixion as an alleged criminal on the accursed tree to be 'Lord and Anointed'; that is, he installed him in his eschatological office as the God-anointed 'Lord' and 'Judge.'"[51] This is not about the adoption of a human figure, but the enthronement of a divine agent with a very definite pre-history in his earthly life, and even pre-existence.[52] The speech therefore describes a "messianic unveiling of what was announced of Jesus in Luke's Gospel right from the start."[53] So Jesus is more properly *known* and *recognized* as Lord and Messiah upon his resurrection rather than transformed into a divine figure by means of resurrection. While a new status and new role is conferred, Jesus's identity, personhood, and being remain consistent upon the resurrection and heav-

---

50. Eskola, *Messiah and the Throne*, 176. Craig S. Keener, *Acts: An Exegetical Commentary*, 4 vols. (Grand Rapids: Baker, 2012–2015], 1:964, says "The language of 'appointing' refers to status, not ontology, and hence is appropriate for Jesus beginning his exaltation."

51. Hengel, *Studies in Early Christology*, 11.

52. Rudolf Pesch, *Apostelgeschichte*, EKKNT (Zürich: Neukirchener Verlage, 1986), 1:128, puts it well: "In [verse] 36, much like Paul's remarks in Rom 1:2f, what shines through is an old traditional Christology of the enthronement of the resurrected Messiah as Son of Man and Son of God. Jesus, the one vindicated by God as the Messiah, does not have his position negated by his crucifixion, but from the moment of his resurrection as 'Lord and Messiah' he has entered into his proper position of power at the right hand of God" (In 36 scheint noch die von Paulus Rom 1,2f aufgenommenen Tradition bezeugte alte Christologie von der Inthronisation des auferwecken Messiasals Menschensohn und Gottesohn durch. Der von Gott als Messias beglaubigte Jesus ist durch seine Kreuzigung nicht widerlegt, sondern seit seiner Auferweckung als 'Herr und Messias' in die ihm zukommende Machtstellung zur Rechten Gottes eingesetzt worden.) See similarly Marshall, *Origins of New Testament Christology*, 119–20; Bates, *Birth of the Trinity*, 161–63; Schröter, *From Jesus to the New Testament*, 233; Eskola, *Messiah and the Throne*, 167.

53. Douglas Buckwalter, *The Character and Purpose of Luke's Christology*, SNTSMS 89 (Cambridge: Cambridge University Press, 1996), 189.

enly ascent. According to Kavin Rowe, the shift to which Acts 2:36 points is not *ontological* but *epistemological*. The adverb "assuredly" (ἀσφαλῶς) and the imperative "let know" (γινωσκέτω) convey the thought that all Israel now has tangible and convincing grounds to reverse its verdict about Jesus because God has reversed everything they did to him by raising him up from death and exalting him to God's right hand. "But" adds Rowe, "God's action (ἐποίησεν ὁ θεός) does not alter Jesus's identity itself; indeed, it *confirms* this identity—precisely as κύριος χριστός."[54] Since the resurrection marks the moment when God enthrones his Son, Israel should now know who Jesus always was: Messiah and Lord.[55]

Conclusion

In light of our study of Rom 1:3–4 and Acts 2:36, it seems improbable that Jesus was ever envisaged as becoming the Son of God at his resurrection. These texts undoubtedly spring from the "first flush of enthusiasm"[56] about Jesus. They do speak of a genuine transformation in Jesus's status. However, this transformation is not from mere human to divine sonship, as much as it is from a messianic role (Son of David) to heavenly regency (Son-of-God-in-power and Lord). Jesus is portrayed as God's chief agent who has been elevated to a position of transcendent status and enjoys a uniquely close connection with God the Father.[57] Yet in this transition, Jesus's divine sonship is presupposed as part of his messianic identity (Rom 1:3–4) and combined with notions of pre-existence and identification of him as "Lord" (Acts 2:36). While Jesus's role as the Son changes, there is no beginning to his divine sonship, as it were.

Moreover, we might note that espousing the exaltation of a human figure to heavenly kingship is distinctly un-Jewish and is not what we might expect to emerge from the Jesus movement in its earliest phase.

54. C. Kavin Rowe, *Early Narrative Christology: The Lord in the Gospel of Luke* (Grand Rapids: Baker, 2009), 194 (italics original).

55. Frank Matera, *New Testament Christology* (Louisville: Westminster John Knox, 1999), 268 n. 44.

56. Dunn, *Beginning from Jerusalem*, 91.

57. Hurtado, *One God, One Lord*, 94–95.

According to Timo Eskola, there is evidence in Jewish literature for exalted patriarchs or angelic figures being ascribed a soteriological function, however, the first Christians were unique in seeing eschatological enthronement as already realized in a Davidic figure, a historical person, for whom the designation "Son" described both his earthly life and his eschatological/soteriological function. Jesus, though exhibiting similar cultic and redemptive powers to other intermediary figures, is different in that he becomes an object of faith and his divine nature is presupposed by his exaltation rather than constituted by it.[58] If anything, passages like Rom 1:3–4 and Acts 2:36 provide a crucial check that whatever might be said of Jesus's status and identity, it must incorporate the mission, passion, and exaltation of Jesus into its discourse.

But where did this come from? A cluster of memory, events, and experiences provided the primary catalyst for most of the christological development that took place in the months and years following Jesus's death: (1) the memory of Jesus's claim to be the messianic agent of Israel's restoration who would share God's throne; (2) the Easter experiences of the disciples; (3) ongoing religious experience, including visions of the risen Jesus; and (4) reflection on Scripture in light of those experiences.[59] It was particularly from the experience of Jesus as risen and exalted and reflecting on Ps 110:1 that we perhaps find the germinal roots of belief in Jesus's pre-existence. Knox, of all people, could even say that pre-existence was implicit in the story from the beginning based on reflection on the post-resurrection status of Jesus.[60] A similar retrojection took place on many

58. Eskola, *Messiah and the Throne*, 173–77. Andrew Chester, *Messiah and Exaltation: Jewish Messianic and Visionary Traditions and New Testament Christology*, WUNT 207 (Tübingen: Mohr Siebeck, 2007), 30, summarizes Eskola this way: "There is some evidence, in Jewish theology and mysticism, for the highest figures in the heavenly world being designated 'gods,' and having a soteriological function, but there is no analogy at all for applying these to a historical figure. Further, exaltation would not itself produce divine features; hence what this suggests is not an adoptionist concept, but that the enthroned one would have had deified status already."

59. Cf. Hurtado, *One God, One Lord*, 114–22; Larry W. Hurtado, *Lord Jesus Christ: Devotion to Jesus in Earliest Christianity* (Grand Rapids: Eerdmans, 2003), 64–74.

60. Knox, *Humanity and Divinity of Christ*, 9–11. On the pre-existence of Jesus in earliest Christianity, that is, before 70 CE, see Simon J. Gathercole, *The Preexistent*

levels, so that Christ's role in eschatology was projected back into the divine protology. Christ's role in soteriology was equated with God's own work in soteriology. It is not hard to imagine how the line of inference went.[61]

If Jesus was "appointed" the Son of God-in-power by his resurrection (Rom 1:4), then he could also have been "appointed the heir of all things" over all of creation (Heb 1:2). If Jesus was the "firstborn from among the dead" (Col 1:18), then one might infer that he also was the "firstborn of all creation" (Col 1:15). If Christ was the harbinger of the new creation (2 Cor 5:17; Rev 21:5), then he must have been the agent who had brought the old creation into being (John 1:3; Col 1:16; 1 Cor 8:6). If Jesus was the "King of kings" (Rev 1:5; 17:14; 19:16), then one could surmise that his kingship and throne stretches back into eternity past and forward into eternity future (Heb 1:8). If the risen Jesus held "all authority on heaven and on earth" (Matt 28:18), then presumably God the Father had given him that authority and dominion from ages past (Mark 2:10; John 5:25; Col 2:10) and into the coming age (Eph 1:21). If Jesus had died "for our sins" (1 John 2:2; 4:10), then of course he was also the "Lamb who was slain from the

---

Son: Recovering the Christologies of Matthew, Mark, and Luke (Grand Rapids: Eerdmans, 2006), 23–45.

61. Sean M. McDonough, *Christ as Creator: Origins of a New Testament Doctrine* (Oxford: Oxford University Press, 2009), 235–36, explains the origins of the doctrine of Christ's agency in creation: "If the one true God worked so evidently, and so dramatically, through his Messiah to sustain and re-create the world (both at the physical and 'spiritual' level), there was every reason to believe the Messiah's mediating role reached back to the very origins of creation. For the early Christians the Messiah was not an afterthought, a kind of cosmic bandage to bind up a broken world, he was God's mode of self-communication to the world from the beginning. . . . The same Messiah who willingly bought back the creation was the one who had brought it into being in the first place." Similar is Richard Bauckham, "Paul's Christology of Divine Identity," in *Oxford Handbook of Pauline Studies*, ed. R. Barry Matlock (Oxford: Oxford University Press, forthcoming): "To include Jesus also in the unique creative activity of God and in the uniquely divine eternity was a necessary corollary of his inclusion in the eschatological identity of God. This was the early Christians' Jewish way of preserving monotheism against the ditheism that any kind of adoptionist Christology was bound to involve. Not by adding Jesus to the unique identity of the God of Israel, but only by including Jesus in that unique identity, could monotheism be maintained." Alternatively see Fletcher-Louis, *Jesus Monotheism*, 141–47, who questions these approaches on the grounds that human figures could be ascribed a role in creation without being divine and human figures could be semi-divine without having a role in creation.

creation of the world" (Rev 13:8). If Jesus is the giver of the Spirit (Luke 24:49; John 7:39; 14:26; 15:26; Acts 1:4–8), then Spirit must be the "Spirit of Jesus Christ" (Phil 1:19; Rom 8:9). If God the Savior redeems through Messiah Jesus (Acts 13:23; 1 Tim 1:1; Jude 25), then Jesus himself can be correlated in a unique way with Israel's God and Savior (Tit 2:12; 2 Pet 1:1).

The premise for this retrojection of Jesus's eschatological role into a role in creation and the equation of Jesus as agent of salvation with the God who saves, is that who Jesus "is" is the same as who he "will be," and who he always "was" (Rev 1:4, 8; 11:17). Or, as the author of Hebrews puts it, "Jesus Christ is the same yesterday and today and forever" (Heb 13:8). A mixture of Easter experience and messianic exegesis meant that Jesus was now to be identified with the God of creation and salvation, not just a thick line between the two; Jesus identified within the divine identity and with the divine actions.

The most powerful catalyst for the origins of Christology and its gradual development into a full-blown incarnationalism was the impression that the man Jesus of Nazareth had upon his disciples that he was God's chief agent in the eschatological scenario of tribulation, deliverance, and consummation. These impressions were reinforced and transformed by their Easter faith, and further spurred on by subsequent religious experiences that were indelibly connected to perceptions of the risen and exalted Jesus's continuing power and presence among his followers. These experiences shaped readings of Scripture. The result gave a grammar to the experiences and further impetus toward verbalizing those experiences in early creeds and preaching. The genetic DNA of the New Testament is not comprised of a single dogma, but of an experience that Jesus lives and reigns. He will reign, for he has always reigned beside God the Father in his purposes and for his glory.[62]

---

62. Ben Witherington, "Jesus as the Alpha and Omega of New Testament Thought," in *Contours of Christology in the New Testament*, ed. Richard N. Longenecker (Grand Rapids: Eerdmans, 2005), 44–45, writes: "What we are dealing with here is a group of people who had had profound religious experiences that they interpreted as encounters with the living Lord – that is, with Jesus the Christ. To be sure, some of their leaders, such as Paul or the author of Hebrews or the Beloved Disciple, could match wits with many of the great minds of their age. But it was their religious experiences with Christ that they had in common. And it was their communities of worship and fellowship,

Viewed from this perspective, an adoptionist Christology proves to be a rather shallow and inadequate expression of the disciples' Easter experiences, post-Easter devotion to Jesus, and immediate reflection about Jesus. The feelings of Jesus's presence, power, and lordship in their religious experience on the one hand, combined with their christologically centered re-reading of Scripture on the other hand, naturally lent itself toward making two inferences: (1) religious experience of the post-earthly Jesus logically registered the question of his pre-existence; and (2) ascent into heaven logically registered the question of a descent from heaven in the first place. Thus, whoever Jesus *is*—Son of God, Messiah, and Lord— he must always *have been* in some form or another![63]

---

which came into being because of those experiences, that provided the matrix for reflection about the meaning of the Christ event." A similar understanding is set out more fully in Luke Timothy Johnson, *Religious Experience in Earliest Christianity: A Missing Dimension in New Testament Study* (Minneapolis: Fortress, 1998).

63. See along these lines William J. Hill, *The Three-Personed God: The Trinity as the Mystery of Salvation* (Washington, DC: Catholic University of America, 1982), 6–7.

CHAPTER 3

The Gospel of Mark, Monotheism, and Deification

Many scholars maintain that the Gospel of Mark, the earliest of the Gospels, has an underdeveloped Christology, lacking the incarnationalism of Paul's letters or John's Gospel. Many have also tried to interpret Mark's Christology against the backdrop of ancient ruler cults and the deification of human beings. It is also alleged that Mark's Gospel contains features representative of an adoptionist Christology, which, particularly in the account of Jesus's baptism, would claim that he descends into the waters as a mere man but rises up as the Son of God. In this chapter, we will see that those assumptions—common though they are—do not stand up to close scrutiny. The Gospel of Mark, taken as a whole, is not congruent with an account of Jesus as a deified human being.

Debates over Markan Christology

Broad recognition of Markan priority in the early twentieth century resulted in increased attention to Mark's Gospel after centuries of relative neglect. Thereafter Markan Christology became a hotbed of controversy. William Wrede's questions about the Markan secrecy motif have dominated research, even if the answers that Wrede gave have long since been abandoned.[1] A theory once fashionable was that Mark's Christology was

1. See Bird, *Are You the One Who Is to Come?*, 66–70.

modelled upon a θεῖος ἀνήρ ("divine man") trope from Hellenistic literature that made Jesus into little more than a miracle-working hero and sage. But the theory faded from scholarly favor when it was realized that there was no fixed and monolithic concept of the "divine man" waiting in the wings to be applied to Jesus.[2] More recently, debates over Markan Christology have revolved around the meaning of the titles of Son of Man and Son of God in light of Mark's narrative and the scriptural backgrounds that determine their meaning. Or else, discussion proceeds over precisely how Jesus embodies royal, prophetic, and priestly roles as the divine agent par excellence.[3] All in all, Mark's Christology presents an intertextually rich and narratively powerful account of Jesus that is unable to satisfy the historical and theological curiosities as to its origins, coherence, and influence.

With regard to the divine sonship of the Markan Jesus, two points require discussion: (1) the placement of the Markan Jesus in evolutionary schemes of early Christology and (2) the general parity of the Markan narrative with accounts of human figures exalted to heaven.

First, the Gospel of Mark is frequently regarded as something of an innovation in the chronology of when and how Jesus became the Son of God. Scholars have assumed a tendency for Christian authors to project Jesus's sonship to an early time, beginning with his resurrection (Rom 1:4; Acts 2:32, 36; 5:30–32; 13:32–33), then earlier at his baptism (Mark 1:9–11), then earlier again at his birth (Matt 1:23; Luke 1:32, 35; Rev 12:5), and even back into eternity (John 1:18; 3:17 ; Rom 8:3; Gal 4:4–5).[4] Consequently, some scholars place Mark within this evolving pattern. Rather than locate Jesus as installed as the Son of God at his resurrection, they interpret Mark

2. See discussion in Gregg S. Morrison, *The Turning Point in the Gospel of Mark: A Study in Markan Christology* (Eugene, OR: Pickwick, 2015), 174–80.

3. See survey in Jacob Chacko Nalupurayil, "Jesus of the Gospel of Mark: Present State of Research," *CurBS* 8 (2000): 191–226; Michael R. Whitenton, *Hearing Kyriotic Sonship: A Cognitive and Rhetorical Approach to the Characterization of Mark's Jesus*, BibInt 148 (Leiden: Brill, 2016), 6–15

4. Weiss, *Earliest Christianity*, 1:123; Raymond E. Brown, *The Birth of the Messiah* (Garden City, NY: Doubleday, 1977), 29–32; Raymond E. Brown, *An Introduction to New Testament Christology* (New York: Paulist Press, 1984), 103–52; Maurice Casey, *From Jewish Prophet to Gentile God: The Origins and Development of New Testament Christology* (Cambridge: James Clarke & Co., 1991), 97–161; Ehrman, *How Jesus Became God*, 236–46.

as affirming that Jesus becomes the Son of God at his baptism, climaxing in a voice from the heavens, "You are my beloved Son, in you I am well pleased!" (Mark 1:11) The Gospel of Mark, so it goes, has no word on Jesus's pre-existence nor a miraculous conception, thus it was during his baptism that Jesus became the Son of God. Note that not merely declared or recognized as God's Son, but literally he was adopted as the Son of God in the Jordan River, which is why he was only then able to proclaim the kingdom, exercise authority over nature, raise the dead, heal the sick, and exorcise demons. According to Ehrman, "Jesus is divine in the sense that he is the one who has been adopted to be the Son of God at his baptism, not later at his resurrection."[5]

Second, scholars continue to debate exactly where Mark's Christology sits on a spectrum between Jewish and Hellenistic beliefs about divine agents. Quite clearly the Gospel of Mark cannot be reduced to the generic category of a Hellenistic etiology of a semi-divine hero, but neither can it be absolutely compartmentalized from Hellenistic literature. On the one hand, Mark's story of Jesus is overwhelmingly shaped by Jewish texts like Dan 7, Pss 2 and 110, as well as Isaiah. As a result, Mark's Gospel is effectively a Greek version of a Jewish-Christian narration about Jesus, the Messiah and Son of God. In other words, Mark is telling a very Jewish story, shaped principally by Jewish Scriptures, and consequently has a very Jewish ambience. If Mark is portraying Jesus as "divine," it will be in a very Jewish way. But on the other hand, Mark's story of Jesus was not written amidst a Judaism that was neatly insulated from Hellenism. Hengel demonstrated—with remarkable success—that Hellenistic Judaism rather than pure paganism shaped Christian constructions of Jesus, so that there was no "syncretistic paganization of primitive Christianity."[6] Be that as it

5. Ehrman, *How Jesus Became God*, 239. See also Julius Wellhausen, *Das Evangelium Marci* (Berlin: G. Reimer, 1903), 7: "In any case, the essential meaning of the baptism of Jesus is found in the fact that it transformed him into the Messiah, he entered into the water as a mere man and came out as the Son of God" (Auf alle Fälle liegt die wesentliche Bedeutung der Taufe Jesu darin, daß sie ihn zum Messias umwandelt, daß er als simpler Mensch in das Wasser hinabsteigt und als der Sohn Gottes wieder heraufkommt).

6. Hengel, *Son of God*, 18. See also James F. McGrath, *The Only True God: Early Christian Monotheism in Its Jewish Context* (Urbana: University of Illinois Press, 2009), 9: "There is nothing within Christianity's doctrine of God in the very earliest period that could not

may, others have labelled this strategy the "Hengel sidestep," which sees any possible influence of Greco-Roman culture on the New Testament as systematically filtered through Hellenistic Judaism, which presumably renders it non-toxic for Christianity.[7] In such a case, Hellenistic Judaism becomes a convenient "buffer" between Christianity and paganism.[8] In actuality the influence of Hellenism could be more direct given that there are various parallels between the Gospels and Hellenistic literature that are just too prominent to ignore.[9] These parallels include the divine portents at the baptism and transfiguration, Jesus's miracle-working abilities, his noble manner of death amidst an otherwise brutal execution, and the disappearance of Jesus's body in tandem with the angelic report of his resurrection. All these features exhibit various degrees of similarity with extant Hellenistic literature.[10] Ancient texts like Mark demonstrate the swirling interface among Jewish, Greek, and Roman texts, traditions, and tropes. Charles Talbert is generally right in his summation of how Christian authors critically absorbed thought forms in Hellenistic culture:

> The earliest followers of Jesus had a distinct constitutive core, experientially grounded, that gave them the ability to sift and sort through language and concepts from their surroundings to express what the Christ event meant to them in terms of their past, present, and future. There was no alien invasion of pagan culture into the pure faith. Rather, there was a sovereign use of the general culture for self-understanding

---

have been taken over from Judaism, nothing that requires us to posit influence of non-Jewish ideas of God within the early Christian community."

7. Luke Timothy Johnson, review of *No One Seeks for God: An Exegetical and Theological Study of Romans 1:18–3:20*, by Richard H. Bell, *RBL* (1999).

8. David Litwa, *Iesus Deus: The Early Christian Depiction of Jesus as a Mediterranean God* (Minneapolis: Fortress, 2014), 16–18.

9. M. Eugene Boring, Klaus Berger, and Carsten Colpe, eds., *Hellenistic Commentary to the New Testament* (Nashville: Abingdon, 1995), esp. 169–81 on Mark's Gospel.

10. We should repeat the caveat that analogy does not mean genealogy and be aware of the danger of "parallelomania," where we endlessly make comparisons between texts and say that this Markan pericope is really just the same as that Homeric unit or that Plutarchian anecdote. Exegesis by parallelism yields an approach that tends to flatten out the distinctive features of texts and treats them as little more than slight variations of a singular literary phenomenon.

and evangelization insofar as it could be adopted to the constitutive, soteriological core.[11]

Taking both hands together, we should be prepared for a complex interface between Jewish and Hellenistic traditions shaping the genre and Christology of Mark's Gospel.

When the Gospel of Mark is compared with Hellenistic literature, many want to read the Gospel as presenting Jesus as a human figure who is *appointed* as God's Son during his lifetime and then, after his death, is *assumed* into heaven and becomes the recipient of divine honors as the enthroned Son of Man. But is this really the case? Does this not require the diminishment of Mark's dense intertextual use of Jewish Scriptures? Is this the conclusion we should reach after a careful reading of Mark's narrative aims and christological claims? For my mind, there are elements of truth here, but also several qualifications and rejoinders that need to be offered.

In light of these debates as to where Mark fits into the development of Christology, and the comparison of Mark with the varied descriptions of deified figures in ancient writings, the rest of this chapter will proceed by: (1) briefly describing ancient views of deification and (2) arguing for the disparity between human deification and an absolutized monotheism. That shows that Mark is unlikely to be a deification story. This in turn prepares us for a close reading of the Markan text as the best way to answer the question as to whether or not Mark contains traces of christological adoptionism.

Exalted Heroes and Deified Emperors in the Greco-Roman World

As mentioned above, there is a long history of identifying parallels between the Markan Jesus and Greco-Roman figures who gain immortality

11. Charles H. Talbert, "The Development of Christology in the First 100 Years: A Modest Proposal," in *The Development of Christology During the First Hundred Years, and Other Essays on Early Christian Christology* (Leiden: Brill, 2011), 41.

and divinity. The comparisons are important because we can only grasp how Jesus is different from other divinized figures like Herakles, Dionysius, Augustus, and Asclepius, once we first see how they are similar. In that sense, a comparative study aids in identifying what is unique and atypical in the presentation of Jesus by the Evangelist. What is periodically suggested is that Mark took up the model of a human figure who is born into the world and who attains divinity because of his mighty exploits.

The possibility that a human being could become a god developed from mythological tales about the divinization of figures like Herakles and, later, Romulus.[12] Subsequently, Hellenistic rulers touted themselves as living images of a god who were then divinized upon death. Alexander the Great (356–323 BCE), who early in his career had begun to represent himself as a son of Zeus and to put himself alongside Herakles, anticipated divinization after his death. Alexander was encouraged by the quasi-worship of himself from his Persian and Egyptian subjects, for whom worship of rulers was quite normal. He himself requested actual worship in Greece and Macedonia.[13] Alexander's cult was quickly established after his early death and, though imitated by his less well-known successors, survived them all. It provided a model and inspiration for the Roman imperial cult in the succeeding centuries.[14]

In the first century CE, Roman emperors and their family members were worshiped as gods during their lifetimes and then formally granted divine honors after their deaths.[15] The introduction of *apotheosis* into Roman religion and politics was far from clear and crisp. Cicero sought to legitimize deification by appeal to traditions about Romulus's assumption; he used the Stoic link between virtue and divinity and pointed to the precedent of Greeks bestowing divine honors on Roman saviors, all while striking a delicate balance between affirming ancestral religion and introducing news ways of venerating an unrivalled political ruler. Roman deification was a classic case of religious hybridity and accordingly became

12. Livy, *Hist.* 1.16; Apollodorus, *Library*, 2.7.7; Cicero, *Off.* 3.25; *Rep.* 2.10.20; *Nat. d.* 2.62; Ovid, *Metam.* 14.812–18.

13. See Arrian, *Anab.* 3.3.2; 4.10.6–7; 7.29.3; Aelian, *Var. hist.* 2.19.

14. N. T. Wright, *The Resurrection of the Son of God*, vol. 3 of *Christian Origins and the Question of God* (London: SPCK, 2003), 55–56.

15. See Appian, *Bell. Civ.* 2.148.

a process riddled with qualifications and ambiguities.[16] During the first decades of the empire, living emperors were not initially worshiped as part of the Roman state cult. Yet, they were still venerated in private cults, in family and neighborhood shrines, and by various associations. There were temples built to the emperor and his family across the provinces, and imperial images were revered all throughout the empire. Some of the emperors were formally deified upon death after a particular process and ceremony. A detailed description of deification is given by Dio Cassius, himself an eyewitness of the funeral rites of the Emperor Pertinax in 193 CE.[17] Augustus had his adoptive father Julius Caesar declared a god, and Tiberius did likewise upon the death of Augustus. The process became ingrained in Roman religion to the point that the Emperor Vespasian is said to have quipped on his death-bed: "Oh dear, I think I am becoming a god."[18] It is important to note that this "divinity" was not merely fictive or political, but was real religious devotion. The emperors, living and deceased, were worshiped since they provided benefaction and benevolence to their subjects who in turn lavished on them the highest honors possible, climaxing in divine acclamation and cultic worship. This imperial divinity was relative rather than absolute. The emperors were not gods like Jupiter or Zeus, but it did not matter. They were gods of the Roman state, and that was all that mattered. It is not surprising that we see the mythology of divinization used to describe emperors like Augustus.[19] In fact, beginning with Augustus, the rank of *princeps* entailed divine sonship, in his case either divinely begotten by Apollo or adopted by the divine Julius. Thereafter, "son of God"—and equivalent expressions—was oriented toward describing a single individual in the empire who had maximal authority, status, power, prestige, and majesty. Vergil wrote about Augustus: "This is he whom you have so often heard promised to you, Augustus Caesar, son of a god [*divi genus*], who shall again set up the Golden Age."[20] In a marble pedestal in Pergamum one finds, "The Emperor, Caesar, son of a god, the

16. Spencer Cole, *Cicero and the Rise of Deification in Rome* (Cambridge: Cambridge University Press, 2013).

17. Dio Cassius, *Hist.* 75.4.2–5.5.

18. Suetonius, *Vesp.* 23.4.

19. Suetonius, *Aug.* 94.4.

20. Vergil, *Aen.* 6.791–793 (Fairclough, LCL).

god Augustus, of every land and sea, the overseer."[21] More contemporary with Paul, some inscriptions describe Nero as "son of the divine Claudius," "son of the divine Augustus," and even "Son of the greatest of the gods, Tiberius Claudius."[22] Evidently Augustus and emperors after him flooded their provinces with media and artwork designed to herald their accomplishments and divine sonship.

We should note a couple of salient features about the divinization of emperors in the imperial cult. First, in the Greco-Roman world, deity was stratified by gradations, so there was a spectrum of divinity. Ascriptions of divinity were not primarily about essence but about honor, status, and power. The chasm between humanity and divinity was traversable for those who achieved great things. This explains why humans can become divine. They are not divine in the same sense as Jupiter or Zeus but enter into a mode of divinity by their virtue and accomplishments. Divine worship did not make someone a god in an absolute sense, only in relation to the worshippers or poets making divine acclamations.[23] A good example of this divine spectrum comes from an inscription, dated to 27 BCE, in the city of Mytilene on the island of Lesbos, where the city council voted the emperor Augustus divine honors. The inscription explains the new honors by which the inhabitants would worship Augustus as a god. It proceeds to promise that "if something more splendid should be found later on, the city's eagerness and piety will not neglect whatever can be done to deify him even more."[24] Mortals could attain divinity and advance in it by virtue of the honors and acclamations that they received from subjects.

Second, worship was the reciprocal response by inhabitants to someone who provided salvation and benefaction. The gods were worshiped

21. Adolf Deissmann, *Light from the Ancient East: The New Testament Illustrated by Recently Discovered Texts of the Graeco-Roman World*, trans. Lionel R. M. Strachan (London: Hodder & Stoughton, 1910), 347.

22. Deissmann, *Light from the Ancient East*, 347.

23. Ittai Gradel, *Emperor Worship and Roman Religion* (Oxford: Clarendon, 2002), 267.

24. Cited in Paul Zanker, *The Power of Images in the Age of Augustus*, trans. Alan Shapiro (Ann Arbor: University of Michigan Press, 1988), 304. See discussion in Michael Peppard, *The Son of God in the Roman World: Divine Sonship in its Social and Political Context* (Oxford: Oxford University Press, 2011), 32–36. See also Philo, *Legat.* 149, who notes that "the whole inhabited world granted honors to him [Augustus] equal to that of the Olympian gods" (my translation).

on the basis that they are not disinterested observers of humanity but genuinely provided aid to them. Cicero said that "[I]f . . . the gods have neither the power nor the will to aid us, if they pay no heed to us at all and take no notice of our actions, if they can exert no possible influence upon the life of men, what ground have we for rendering any sort of worship, honor or prayer to the immortal gods?"[25] The same deal of worship in return for benefits was applied to human figures. Plutarch records that the Roman plebs erected shrines and offered sacrifices as for a god to the Gracchi brothers, tribunes of the republican era, who undertook important reforms for the rural poor.[26] A decree from Croan says that "Since Emperor Caesar, son of God, god Sebastos, has by his benefactions to all men outdone even the Olympian gods."[27] Philo could praise Caligula as the "Savior and Benefactor who was expected to pour down fresh and everlasting springs of blessings upon all of Asia and Europe."[28] While Philo was allergic to ascribing divinity to Caligula, he did not hold back in the praises that practically amounted to divinity: adulation for salvation and benefaction. The underlying premise seems to be that what makes someone a "god" is not who they are, but what they have done for you. John White sums it up well: "Good rulers were divinized for the same reason that gods were worshiped: they were acknowledged as saviors of the social order."[29] Saving a province from barbarian invasion, tyrannical rule, famine, civil war, or such, could meet with a response of divine worship with the building of temples, altars, and offering sacrifices. Offering worship implied an obligation of benefaction incumbent upon a ruler in the form of tax-relief, the promise of security, the hosting of games, and the like. Benefaction resulted in worship, and continuous benefaction resulted in continuous worship.[30] We see clear examples of this in first-century literature. Vergil wrote that the Augustus was "a god who wrought for us this peace—for a god he shall ever be to me; often

25. Cicero, *Nat. d.* 1.3 (Rackham, LCL).
26. Plutarch, *Ti. C. Gracch.* 18.
27. *I. Olympia* 53 cited in Whitenton, *Kyriotic Sonship*, 111.
28. Philo, *Legat.* 22 (my translation).
29. John L. White, *The Apostle of God: Paul and the Promise of Abraham* (Peabody, MA: Hendrickson, 1999), 99.
30. Cf. Peppard, *Son of God in the Roman World*, 40.

shall a tender lamb from our folds stain his altar."[31] Not to be outdone, Horace said of Augustus: "Thunder in heaven confirms our faith—Jove rules there; but here on earth Augustus shall be hailed as god also, when he makes new subjects of the Britons and the dour Parthians."[32] Augustus is a great god because he does great things for the people.[33]

Divinity here is primarily about status while cultic worship is the reciprocal response from those who enjoy the emperor's benefits. In other words, the highest form of patronage required the highest form of praise in return, namely, divine worship.

Monotheism and Divinized Humans

Before we accede to the notion that Christ devotion was modelled on deified figures, we should countenance Greco-Roman critiques of divinization, note the incongruity of human deification with Jewish monotheism, and observe what Christian authors said about comparisons of the Jesus story with the deification of human figures. This will provide a useful caveat about the inability to square the divinization of emperors with Mark's Christology.

Greco-Roman Doubts about Deification

The notion of worship directed toward a living ruler who was then deified upon death was open to crude criticism and even sardonic satire. On liv-

31. Vergil, *Ecl.* 1.6–8 (Fairclough, LCL).
32. Horace, *Carm.* 3.5 (Michie, LCL).
33. We should note a minority position attributed to the Epicureans whereby "deity possesses an excellence and pre-eminence which must of its own nature attract the worship of the wise" (Cicero, *Nat. d.* 1.115–16 [Rackham, LCL]). The idea that deified emperors had intrinsic divinity was commended in places; for instance, Seneca said of Augustus, "We believe him to be a god, but not because we are ordered to do so" (*Clem.* 1.10.3 [Basore, LCL]), and Pliny contrasts Trajan's piety with that of his predecessors: "You gave your father [Nerva] his place among the stars with no thought of terrorizing your subjects, of bringing the gods into disrepute, or of gaining reflected glory, but simply because you thought he was a god" (*Pan.* 11.2 [Radice, LCL]).

ing rulers, Alexander's demand that Greece recognize him as a god was met with derisive complicity with the Spartan Damis laconically stating: "Since Alexander wants to be a god, let him be a god."[34] The Cynic philosopher Diogenes derided Alexander's deification with notable sarcasm: "When the Athenians gave Alexander the title of Dionysus, he said, 'Me too you might make Serapis.'"[35] Tacitus sneered at Augustus's pretentiousness and appetite for divine praise: "No honor was left for the gods, when Augustus chose to be himself worshiped with temples and statues, like those of the deities, and with flamens and priests."[36] On deification, in Cicero's treatise *On the Nature of Gods*, the philosopher Cotta attacked the very idea, blasting "those who teach that brave or famous or powerful men have been deified after death, and that it is these who are the real objects of the worship, prayers, and adoration to which we are accustomed to offer."[37] The enrolling of human figures into celestial citizenship becomes "a sort of extension of the franchise" of divinity.[38] At the most, the hope of "divine honors" was for the "purpose of promoting valor, to make the best men more willing to encounter danger for their country's sake."[39] It was one thing to believe in the immortal souls of famous men, but quite another that deified heroes could return to assist the legions in battle.[40] Dio Cassius is positively dripping with disdain when he describes the supposed deification of Caligula's mistress Drusilla as the goddess Panthea.[41] Lucian of Samosata describes how he comically ignited the rumor that the self-seeking philosopher Peregrinus ascended to heaven after his self-immolation.[42] The system of deification was already sufficiently established to be lampooned by Seneca on the death of Claudius in Seneca's famous book about the *Pumpkinification* of Claudius. The story includes a mockery of the whole process of deification with the

---

34. Plutarch, *Mor.* 219 (Babbitt, LCL).
35. Diog. Laert. 6.2.63 (Hicks, LCL).
36. Tacitus, *Ann.* 1.10 (Moore, LCL).
37. Cicero, *Nat. d.* 1.119 (Rackham, LCL).
38. Cicero, *Nat. d.* 3.39 (Rackham, LCL).
39. Cicero, *Nat. d.* 3.50 (Rackham, LCL).
40. Cicero, *Nat. d.* 3.11–12.
41. Dio Cassius, *Hist.* 59.11.4.
42. Lucian, *Peregr.* 38–42.

gods debating whether Claudius should be admitted to their company; they decide against it. In the satire, Janus complains, "At one time, it was a great thing to be made a god, but now you have made the distinction a farce. So that my remarks do not seem to be directed at a particular individual, rather than the issue, I propose that from this day onwards no one shall be made a god from those who eat the fruits of the earth or whom the fruitful earth nourishes."[43] Ittai Gradel grasps the point of the story: "Humans can, according to Seneca, elevate a man to heaven; only the gods, however, decide if he will actually be admitted."[44] Seneca's story dovetails with Plutarch's oblique criticism of deification, using Romulus as the example but probably having in mind contemporary Roman practices. Truth and right reason, urged Plutarch, demanded that one is not made a god by civic pronouncement, but a virtuous soul may evolve from human to hero to demi-god and, after purification, into a god in an absolute sense.[45] The political fiction involved in deification was exploited by Christian apologists like Minucius Felix, who said that the deification of Romulus and Juba was "not on account of belief in their divinity, but in honor of the power that they exercised."[46] In the end, deification had meaning within the symbolic world of the imperium, but it was also a contested process. Whether an emperor would be deified was one question (Tiberius, Caligula, and Domitian were not deified), the evidence for deification was mooted (portents and witnesses were required, but often contrived), and honors were not consistent (they ranged from mere divine title to full-scale temple with priesthood, and even then cults could lapse from disuse).[47] As Beard, North, and Price note: "Every narrative of Roman apotheosis tells, at the same time, a story of uncertainty, challenge, debate and mixed motives."[48] Deification involved a composite of mythical storytelling, public ritual, and political negotiation and became

43. Seneca, *Apoc.* 9 (Warmington, LCL).
44. Gradel, *Emperor Worship and Roman Religion*, 329.
45. Plutarch, *Rom.* 28.8.
46. Minucius Felix, *Oct.* 21 (Wallis, *ANF* [amended]). Plutarch, *Alex.* 28.6, said that Alexander used belief in his divinity for the subjugation of others.
47. Gradel, *Emperor Worship and Roman Religion*, 345.
48. Mary Beard, John North, and Simon Price, *Religions of Rome*, 2 vols. (Cambridge: Cambridge University Press, 1998), 1:148.

"a process that involves fraud *and* piety, tradition *and* contrived novelty, political advantage *and* religious truth."[49]

Part of the reason for rejecting deification was because some authors did absolutize divinity. Divinity in Greco-Roman religion was a spectrum. One could be divine *in relation to* a group of worshippers. Yet, there remained fundamental differences between humans and the eternal gods.[50] The differences were such that, even within the spectrum of divinity, there was a point of exclusion for mortals, an absolute difference between the eternal gods and those who attained divinity by merit. This is manifested in the scheme where there were two classes of gods: the eternals and human immortals installed in heaven by merit.[51] Cicero's Cotta saw the divine form—and form is a mixture of species and status—as prior and superior to the human form, with the human form a lesser copy of the divine, saying, "the gods did not derive the pattern of their form from men; since the gods have always existed, and were never born—that is, they are to be eternal; whereas men were born; therefore the human form existed before mankind; and it was the form of the immortal gods."[52] Philo lambasted Caligula because in his presentation of himself "he went beyond the demigods, and dared to rehearse and usurp the worship offered to the greater deities of the world, Mercury, and Apollo, and Mars."[53] Philo, even as a Jewish observer, could tell that for a pagan emperor, this was horribly impious. The premise behind deification was that there were different types

49. Beard, North, and Price, *Religions of Rome*, 1:149 (italics original).

50. According to Cicero (*Nat. d.* 3.39–50), the spectrum of divinity was also a problem because if humans, animals, islands, virtues, and planetary objects are divine, then divinity becomes so widespread that it loses its currency and has little differentiation from ordinary existence.

51. Diodorus Siculus, *Library* 6.1.2 (Oldfather, LCL): "As regards the gods, men of ancient times have handed down to later generations two different conceptions: Certain of the gods, they say, are eternal and imperishable . . . for each of these genesis and duration are from everlasting to everlasting. But the other gods, we are told, were terrestrial beings who attained to immortal honors and fame because of their benefactions to mankind, such as Heracles, Dionysus, Aristaeus, and the others who were like them." See also Diodorus Siculus, *Library* 4.1.4; Cicero, *Leg.* 2.19; Plutarch, *Pel.* 16.5; Philo, *Legat.* 93; Quintilian, *Inst.* 3.7.9.

52. Cicero, *Nat. d.* 1.90 (Rackham, LCL).

53. Philo, *Legat.* 93 (translation mine).

of "divinity" because there were different ways of becoming divine. There were differences between being honored as a god, being decreed a god, being made a god, and being eternally and unchangeably divine. For all the emphasis upon relative rather than absolute divinity in recent scholarship, the Romans saw an absolute distinction between men and the gods. The distinction was fundamental to *auspicia* and *sacrificia*, what was offered by the deity and the cultic devotion that was returned. According to Michael Koortbojian, "while the performance of these rites may well have required merely a sense of 'relative' power distinctions, their success and the *beneficia* they brought forth were predicated on the 'absolute' power of those gods to whom the rites appealed."[54] This is why deceased emperors were ranked last of all in quality of sacrifices they were offered, behind the traditional gods and even behind the living emperor. The sacrifices made by the Arval Brothers, a college of Roman priests, to both traditional gods and to the imperial family, indicates the ranking of deities. A major sacrifice consisting of a bull was made to the *genius* of the living emperor and to major male gods (e.g., Mars, Apollo), while a cow was offered to female divinities (e.g., Juno, Minerva), and a minor sacrifice consisting of a castrated steer was offered to a *divus*, or deified emperor. The deities were ranked and that ranking was expressed in sacrifice and ritual.[55] Although the *divi* were divine and received sacrifice, they were not on par with the traditional gods in terms absolute power and status, which is why they received a lesser sacrifice—they were different in nature.

We see something of absolute divinity in the way that Roman emperors either tip-toed or encroached upon the divine status of Jupiter. In 44 BCE, during a prominent festival, the serving consul, Mark Antony, presented Julius Caesar with a diadem, urging him to take it and to declare himself king. The suggestion was flabbergasting and audacious because Rome had long since associated kings with tyranny and had expelled the last king of Rome centuries earlier. Even worse, Jupiter was meant to be Rome's only sovereign. Caesar's response to Antony's invitation,

---

54. Michael Koortbojian, *The Divinization of Caesar and Augustus: Precedents, Consequences, Implications* (Cambridge: Cambridge University Press, 2013), 23–24; contrasted with Peppard, *Son of God in the Roman World*, 31.

55. Gradel, *Emperor Worship and Roman Religion*, 275–76; Koortbojian, *The Divinization of Caesar and Augustus*, 126.

undoubtedly staged, was to refuse the diadem and Caesar insisted that it be placed instead in the temple of Jupiter.[56] Just as zealous Judeans could say that Israel had no king but God,[57] so too could the Romans say that they had no king but Jupiter Optimus Maximus, king of the gods and the Romans.[58] Philo regarded it as an abomination that Caligula intended to put a statue of himself in the Jerusalem temple inscribed with the name *Dios* for "Zeus."[59] During a triumphal procession, the triumphator would dress in the costume of Jupiter,[60] a display that was meant to announce the prowess of the general and the power of Jupiter over Rome's affairs. The triumphator was a living image of Jupiter in the ceremony, but was not Jupiter per se, and was told "Look behind you. Remember, you are only a man" by an attendant accompanying him in his chariot.[61] In Ovid's *Metamorphoses* the emperor is the highest ruler but still second to Jupiter, who has ultimate authority on deifications.[62] Coinage from the time of Nero shows Nero's image juxtaposed with Jupiter, indicating Jupiter's sponsorship of Nero's regime.[63] Such allergy to usurping the divinity of Jupiter was not shared by all Roman rulers. Various statues and reliefs from the Julio-Claudian period show that not only the living emperor but also the deified emperor was to be regarded as Jupiter's earthly parallel, so as to liken the emperor to the most illustrious of Roman gods in terms of his power and authority.[64] Gaius Caligula routinely attired himself as one of the gods, including Jupiter, and earned the scorn of later writers.[65] While cultivating divine honors was acceptable, usurping the

---

56. Cicero, *Phil.* 2.34; 3.5; Suetonius, *Jul.* 79.2.

57. Josephus, *A.J.* 18.23.

58. Livy, *Hist.* 1.53; Dio Cassius, *Hist.* 44.11.3.

59. Philo, *Legat.* 188.

60. Pliny the Elder, *Nat.* 33.111–12; 35.157; Livy, *Hist.* 10.7.9.

61. Tertullian, *Apol.* 33.4, though whether this was a permanent fixture of a triumph is unlikely; see Mary Beard, *The Roman Triumph* (London: Belknap, 2009), 85–92.

62. Ovid, *Metam.* 15.840–41, 858–60.

63. See Mark Reasoner, *Roman Imperial Texts: A Sourcebook* (Minneapolis: Fortress, 2013), 231–32.

64. Koortbojian, *Divinization of Caesar and Augustus*, 214. Minucius Felix (*Oct.* 21 [Wallis, *ANF*]) commented that "the monstrous appearances of Jupiter are as numerous as his names."

65. Suetonius, *Cal.* 52; Dio Cassius, *Hist.* 59.26.6–9; Philo, *Legat.* 75–114.

divine honors of the traditional gods was often not, as Tacitus' comment about Augustus suggests.[66]

The practice of humans becoming gods was doubted and derided by many. However, it was also real to many, real within the symbolic universe created by a cultus, even if there were limits to which humans could ascend. What all this means is that the author of Mark's Gospel, while absorbing features of Hellenistic literature, cannot be assumed to be going along with divinization and using it as a model to apply to Jesus. The process of divinization was open to question and ridicule, especially by those whose own view of monotheism was more absolutized than those who saw divine status primarily as an extension of earthly political power.

Jewish Denunciation of Human Deification

Rome exported the cult of the emperors. The cult served to focus the loyalty of the provinces on the imperial *persona*. Expressing loyalty to the imperium through building temples was both required from the top down and enthusiastically requested from the bottom up.[67] Jewish religious scruples prohibited the use of images and the worship of human figures, meaning that Judean and Diasporan communities could not participate in this process of imperial benefaction in exchange for divine honors. The Roman response to indigenous religions was largely to respect the ancestral customs (*mos maiorum*). This was certainly the case for the Jews under the Republic and even into the early empire.[68] The Jews were able to negotiate the imperial cult by a mixture of strategies. These strategies included participation in the imperial cult as typified by Herod the Great, who ringed Palestine with imperial temples and monuments.[69] Alternatively, several gestures of loyalty were able to substitute for offering sac-

---

66. Tacitus, *Ann.* 1.10.

67. Peter Garnsey and Richard P. Saller, *The Roman Empire: Economy, Society and Culture* (London: Duckworth, 1987), 164–65.

68. Cf. Josephus, *A.J.* 14.259–60; 16.162–65; 19.289–91.

69. See Monika Bernett, *Der Kaiserkult in Judaä unter den Herodiern und Römern: Untersuchungen zur politischen und religiösen Geschicht Judaäs von 30 v. bis 66 n. Chr.*, WUNT 203 (Tübingen: Mohr Siebeck, 2007).

rifices to the emperor, such as offering sacrifices in the Jerusalem temple on behalf of the emperor,[70] offering prayers for the welfare of the imperial family,[71] and taking oaths of loyalty to the emperor.[72] The Jews of Palestine and the Diaspora adapted to honoring the emperor within the parameters of their customs and cultic traditions.[73] However, what most Jews could not broach—notwithstanding persons like Tiberius Alexander and political pragmatists like Herod the Great—was veneration of divine images and worship of a human figure.[74] It was the nature of Israel's one God and the type of worship that this God required that ruled out Jewish subjects venerating deified human figures.

Turning to the subject of Jewish monotheism, we come to a disputed topic. Whether there even was such a thing as "monotheism" in the ancient world or even in the Hebrew Scriptures is open to discussion.[75] Then there is the question as to whether Jewish monotheism was "strict" or "inclusive," that is, inclusive in the sense that other beings could share in divinity and worship besides Yahweh. According to Richard Bauckham, a survey of biblical and post-biblical texts reveals that Jewish monotheism conceptualized God's unique identity in three things: (1) God's sacred name, Yahweh, revealed to Israel; (2) God's sovereignty over all things as creator; and (3) the exclusive worship he commanded. To be brief, in this dominant species of Jewish monotheism, there is one

70. Philo, *Legat.* 157; Josephus, *C. Ap.* 2.77.

71. Philo, *Flacc.* 48–50; *Legat.* 133.

72. Josephus, *A.J.* 17.42.

73. Bruce W. Winter, *Divine Honours for the Caesars: The First Christians' Responses* (Grand Rapids: Eerdmans, 2015), 112 (the whole section in pages 94–123 is an informative read).

74. See Philo, *Legat.* 346; Josephus, *A.J.* 19.304–6; *B.J.* 2.184–85.

75. See, e.g., Walter Moberly, "How Appropriate is 'Monotheism' as a Category for Biblical Interpretation?" in *Early Jewish and Christian Monotheism*, ed. Loren T. Stuckenbruck and Wendy E. S. North, JSNTSup 263 (London: T&T Clark. 2004), 216–34, and Paula Fredriksen, "Mandatory Retirement: Ideas in the Study of Christian Origins Whose Time Has Come to Go," in *Israel's God and Rebecca's Children: Christology and Community in Early Judaism and Christianity. Essays in Honor of Larry W. Hurtado and Alan F. Segal*, ed. David B. Capes, April D. DeConick, Helen K Bond, and Troy A. Miller (Waco, TX: Baylor University Press, 2007), 35–38. In contrast, McGrath, *The Only True God*, 23–37, accepts the appropriateness of the term "monotheism" for describing Jewish devotion, but characterizes it as a highly flexible monotheism.

Creator God, YHWH, who stands above all other reality. He covenants with Israel, with a demand for aniconic and monolatrous worship, worship of the one true God to exclusion of all others.[76] Chris Tilling presses further, agreeing with Bauckham that Israel's God was in a transcendent class of his own. Wanting to sharpen the set of relationships that typified Yahweh's relationship with Israel and the requirements for worshippers, Tilling stresses how God is: (1) the object of ultimate goals, such as glory; (2) the recipient of ardent devotion, including cultic worship; (3) experienced as an active and present power while simultaneously resident in heaven; (4) the author of communication between heaven and earth; and (5) often described in unique and superlative forms in terms of his character and the nature of his lordhip. For Tilling, while one might detect an intermediary figure who shares part or some of these qualities or relationalities; nonetheless, he notes that "the complete *pattern* remains descriptive of the God-relation alone."[77]

Still, the issue remains whether God's own "divinity" is really unique or communicable, absolute or gradated, exclusive or inclusive. We can easily find Jewish literature referring to heavenly beings who seem to represent and stand in for Israel's God, including the Angel of the Lord.[78] The angel Metratron functions as a heavenly vice-regent.[79] Philo calls the Logos a "second god."[80] The Enochic Son of Man is a heavenly figure who receives homage.[81] Or else human figures are treated with divine status and given divine tasks like Adam,[82] Enoch,[83] and Moses,[84] and in

---

76. Bauckham, *Jesus and the God of Israel*, 1–106. For critiques of Bauckham, see esp. Chris Tilling, *Paul's Divine Christology* (Grand Rapids: Eerdmans, 2012), 11–62. Tilling complains that "Bauckham's own categories of identifying the unique divine identity are not always maintained in Second Temple literature, nor is it likely that a free-floating set of categories concerning God's relation to all reality was as decisive in the minds of these Jews as he maintains" (61).

77. Tilling, *Paul's Divine Christology*, 240 (italics original).

78. See, e.g., Gen 16:13; 21:17–18; 22:11–12; Judg 2:1.

79. *3 En.* 4.5; 10.3–6; 12.1–5.

80. Philo, *QG* 2.62.

81. 1 En. 48.1–7; 51.3; 61.8.

82. LAE 12–16.

83. 2 En. 22.1–10.

84. Sir 45.1–5; Philo, *Sacr.* 9–10; *Mos.* 1.27, 155–58; 2.288–92.

the Qumran scrolls Melchizedek exercises the divine prerogative of judgment and is even called Elohim ("god") in the sense of Ps 82.[85] In several Jewish texts, humans could experience post-mortem transformations into glorious states and attain angelic qualities. Yet, they seem to fall short of a deification that gives them equality with Yahweh in power and being.[86] Many have naturally seen in these intermediary figures clear evidence that divinity was inclusive rather than exclusive and regarded them as an explanation for describing how divinity was acquired by or attributed to Jesus.

To my mind, none of the things said about intermediary figures disproves that many Jews were strict monotheists, nor do they comprise an obvious paradigm for how a human figure like Jesus can be regarded as a divine person. The description of intermediary figures in the literature demonstrates a certain tension and a need in Jewish thought to account for: (1) how the one God of heaven is immanent and interactive with creation; and (2) how humanity will triumph over evil and reign over creation as the Scriptures appear to imply. The intermediary figures occupy roles that partly resolve those tensions but also raise a host of new questions about who are they in relation to God and the limits of humans attaining divine qualities. In addition, the intermediary figures do present genuine analogues that resemble the descriptions and narratives about Jesus in Christian sources. However, stark differences stand out as well: no one seems to major on Ps 110 as an inspiration; there is a distinctive narrative about a pre-existent figure coming to earth and a human figure exalted to heaven; messianism is enjoined with mysticism about sharing a divine throne; plus an unprecedented blend of scriptural imagery drawn from Genesis, Isaiah, Daniel, and the Psalms—while no single element is entirely unique, the christological discourse of the New Testament taken as a whole lacks precise parallel.

At the risk of oversimplification, I am convinced that Jewish monotheism was generally strict.[87] Undoubtedly, some Jews had a conception

85. 11Q13 2.9–13.
86. See Chester, *Messiah and Exaltation*, 61–80.
87. See further, Hurtado, *Lord Jesus Christ*, 29–52; Larry W. Hurtado, "First-Century Jewish Monotheism," *JSNT* 71 (1998): 3–26; Larry W. Hurtado, "Monotheism, Principal Angels, and the Background of Christology," in *The Oxford Handbook of the*

of God with flexible boundaries for divinity, perhaps lacking consistency, reflecting hybridity between Jewish and Hellenistic perspectives on deities, and exhibiting varied views on the relationship of intermediary figures to Israel's God—hence, the emergence of the "two powers in heaven" heresy.[88] Other Jews could exhibit a pluralistic monotheism with the one sovereign God of creation, Yahweh, manifested in different religions under a different name like Zeus or Dios.[89] And again, other Jews were consciously pluralistic and often participated in pagan cults, some engaged in syncretistic practices, and others were at least tolerant of pagan religions.[90] All of which is a far cry from the mockery and contempt toward idolatry in some Jewish writings.[91] With those caveats in mind, it appears to me that the Jewish monotheism reflected in the New Testament and in Second Temple Jewish literature more generally tends to absolutize the distinction between God on the one hand and lesser heavenly beings and the created world on the other hand. While there are heavenly and supernatural beings such as angels and spirits, and although exalted human

---

Dead Sea Scrolls, ed. Timothy H. Lim and John J. Collins (Oxford: Oxford University Press, 2010), 546–64; Larry W. Hurtado, "'Ancient Jewish Monotheism' in the Hellenistic and Roman Periods," *Journal of Ancient Judaism* 4 (2013): 379–400; and Bauckham, *Jesus and the God of Israel*.

88. For an update about this debate, see McGrath, *The Only True God*, 81–96.

89. In a piece of Jewish apologetic literature we read: "These [Jewish] people worship God the overseer and creator of all, whom all men worship including ourselves, O King, except we have a different name. Their name for him is Zeus and Jove" (Let. Arist. 15). The Roman Marcus Terentius Varro regarded the "God of the Jews to be the same as Jupiter" (Augustine, *Cons.* 1.22.30).

90. A number of inscriptions found in the vicinity of a temple complex at el-Kanais in Egypt are dedicated to "Pan of the Successful Journey" and can be dated ca. 150–180 BCE. One of them features a Jewish supplicant: "Ptolemaios [son] of Dionysios, a Jew, blesses the god." The cult of the "Most High God" in northern Asia Minor and the ubiquity of magical amulets and papyri with Jewish themes is evidence for some expressions of Jewish syncretism. Also, a clear instance of respect for pagan religion is found in the Septuagint translation of Exod 22:27 that changes "You shall not curse *God*" in the singular to "You shall not curse *gods*" in the plural—an attitude affirmed by both Philo, *Mos.* 2.205, and Josephus, *A.J.* 4.207, in urging Jews not to insult Greco-Roman religions.

91. E.g., Isa 44:9–20, Wis 11–15, Let. Arist. 132–71, Jub. 22.17–18, Josephus, *C. Ap.* 2.167, 190–91. In the New Testament: 1 Thess 1:9; Gal 5:20; 1 Cor 8–10; 12:2; 2 Cor 6:16; 1 Pet 4:3; 1 John 5:21; Rev 2:14, 20; 9:20; 21:8; 22:15.

figures are often treated inclusively within divine activity and receive a type of obeisance, they do not encroach on God's ultimate power and superlative status.

One should be generally impressed with how this scheme accounts for Jewish texts and tradition in the Second Temple period.[92] The Shema, the famous prayer that all faithful Jews are meant to recite every day, provided the baseline for an exclusive monotheism, "Hear, O Israel: The LORD our God, the LORD is one."[93] We see the same thing in a prayer from the second century BCE recalling Nehemiah's words at the resumption of sacrifices in the temple: "O Lord, Lord God, Creator of all things, you are awe-inspiring and strong and just and merciful, you alone are king and are kind, you alone are bountiful, you alone are just and almighty and eternal."[94] In *Aristeas* the high priest Eleazar announces that "God is one, that his power is shown in everything, every place being filled with his sovereignty."[95] Josephus reports that "God as one is common to all the Hebrews."[96] Philo, who could refer to Moses as "God and King of the whole nation" and call the Logos a "second God," yet still touted strict comprehensively monotheistic principles: "Therefore, of first importance, let us inscribe in ourselves this first commandment as the holiest of all commandments, to think that there is but one God, the most high, and to honor him alone; and do not permit polytheistic doctrine to even touch the ears of any person who is accustomed to seek after the truth, with a clean and pure of heart."[97] What is more, Jews were perceived by Romans to be strange and even atheistic precisely on account of their monotheistic devotion, so much so that the historian Tacitus could comment that "the Jews conceive of one god alone."[98] Note the emphasis in these texts: God is one, God alone, and one God. That is

92. See also Jdt 5:6–8; 2 Macc 1:24–25; 7:37; 3 Macc 5:13; Let. Arist. 132, 139; Jos. Asen. 11.10; Sib. Or. 3.629; Josephus, *A.J.* 3:91; 4:201; 5:112; 8:335–37, 343; 18:23; *B.J.* 7.410; *C. Ap.* 2:193; Philo, *Decal.* 65; Ps.-Orph., *Orphica* 10–12.

93. Deut 6:4; cf. Deut 11:13–21; Num 15:37–41.

94. 2 Macc 1:24–25.

95. Let. Arist. 132 (Shutt, *OTP*).

96. Josephus, *A.J.* 5.112 (Thackeray and Marcus, LCL).

97. Philo, *Decal.* 65 (my translation).

98. Tacitus, *Hist.* 5.5.4 (LCL).

not to say that every Jew accepted this axiom and lived by it consistently all the time. We have good evidence that many did not, with many Jews acculturating themselves to Greco-Roman religion in varying degrees. However, all things being equal, we can detect a clear, crisp, and sharp belief that Israel's God was thought to be the creator of all, Israel's God was unique among all claimants to divinity, and Israel's God is and will be king over all.[99]

We see how this monotheism plays out in Jewish critiques of Caligula's claims to divinity.[100] Josephus, the Jewish Pharisee turned Roman collaborator, could laud Caligula for the magnanimity exercised in the early years of his reign and praise his moderation. "But," Josephus adds, "as time went on, he ceased to think of himself as a man and, as he imagined himself a god because of the greatness of his empire, he was moved to disregard the divine power in all his official acts."[101] According to John Barclay: "Josephus insists on a clear distinction between humanity and God, with the implication that even emperors cannot cross this line."[102] Elsewhere Josephus apologetically explains Jewish exclusive devotion to God and their disregard for idol worship with particular emphasis on how it relates to honors for the emperor. Josephus argues that God's purpose in prohibiting the worship of idols was not to dishonor Roman authority, but premised on the notion that worshipping images lacked necessity and utility. He treads a fine line in describing how the exclusive devotion of Jews to their God does not prohibit them from offering honors to the emperors and people of Rome. Josephus declares: "[O]ur legislator, not in order to put, as it were, a prophetic veto upon honors paid to the Roman authority, but out of contempt for a practice profitable to neither God nor man, forbade the making of images, alike any living creature, and much more of God, who, as is shown later on, is not a creature."[103] Two key things emerge from this: first, Josephus expresses the view of an unbridgeable divide between God and human beings that rules out deification; second, that

99. Wright, *Paul and the Faithfulness of God*, 620–21.
100. See esp. Philo, *Legat.* 200–3; Josephus, *A.J.* 18.257–58.
101. Josephus, *Ant.* 18.256 (Feldman, LCL).
102. John Barclay, *Flavius Josephus: Against Apion* (Leiden: Brill, 2007), 208.
103. Josephus, *C. Ap.* 2.76 (Thackeray, LCL).

human beings might be fitting subjects of honor but they should not receive God-worship.

We find more or less the same thing in Philo.[104] The Jewish philosopher of Alexandria was involved in the petition to urge Caligula to end the pogrom against Jews in the city and to renege on his intention to place a statue of himself in the Jerusalem temple. Philo clearly regarded Caligula's pretentions to divinity to be emblematic of his unrestrained megalomania. He said that Caligula "no longer chose to remain confined by the ordinary limits of human nature, but was fervent to raise himself above all others, and supposed himself to be a god . . . that he should be considered a person of a superior type, and not merely human, but one who has received a greater portion of divinity."[105] Caligula was deluded to the point that he did not only call himself a god, but really believed he was a god."[106] For Philo this all amounted to a form of religious deviancy based on Caligula's "godless deification" (ἀθεωτάτην ἐκθέωσιν).[107] Caligula does not live up to Roman mythology, for the sons of Jupiter, Castor and Pollux, attained celestial immortality on account of their virtue, for virtue is what bequeaths immortality for men just as vice changes the immortals into mortals.[108] More forcefully, Philo stresses an absolute distinction between divinity and humanity, since "the form of God is not something like money which is so easily replicated by an inferior type."[109] Caligula can masquerade as Mars all he likes, but "he is fundamentally different to Mars in every respect of being and action . . . [so] that Gaius [Caligula] ought not be compared to any god, not even to any demi-god, since he has neither the same nature, nor the same essence, nor the same purposes as them."[110] The rationale for rejecting Caligula's self-deification is that the spectacle is cosmetic rather than cosmic, rhetorical rather than real, and

---

104. There are antecedents in Alexandrian Judaism for Philo's critique of human divinization in Let. Arist. 140 that regards the title "men of God" or "divine men" (ἀνθρώπους θεοῦ) as unsuitable for mere mortals, and better describes those who worship God according to the truth.

105. Philo, *Legat.* 75–76 (my translation).

106. Philo, *Legat.* 162 (my translation).

107. Philo, *Legat.* 77 (my translation).

108. Philo, *Legat.* 84, 91.

109. Philo, *Legat.* 110 (my translation).

110. Philo, *Legat.* 112, 114 (my translation).

vain rather than virtuous. Philo is unwilling to go along with the pretense because he belongs to the pious and learned race who "profess that there is one God, their Father and the Creator of the world."[111] Philo believed in the comparative superiority of priesthood over kingship in the same way that "God is superior to humanity; for humanity renders service to God, while God has the responsibility of governing them."[112] The ontological distinction between God and humanity and the impiety of trying to usurp divine honors for oneself entails that incarnation and divinization are categorically impossible. Philo thus adds his parenthetical comment: "Sooner could God change into a man than a man into God."[113]

If we bring Josephus and Philo together in their critiques of deification, then we can agree with Dunn that, "Jewish writings tend to be more scrupulous and less free in their attribution of divine sonship and divinity to men."[114] The premise of monotheism, even with subordinate and intermediary figures, includes an absolute distinction between God and humanity that could not be traversed.

So, if Jewish monotheism was generally strict, erecting a divide between God and humanity, and prohibiting deification as well as divine honors for mortals, then what are we to make of intermediary figures like the Angel of the Lord or exalted patriarchs such as Adam, Enoch, and Moses? Do they go against this grain of strict monotheism? I am inclined to say "no." Jewish authors could easily accept the notion of "subordinate powers" through whom God acted to create, reveal, and redeem without in any way compromising this strict monotheism.[115] These intermediary beings were necessary for imagining how a transcendent deity can work immanently within the world, but without necessarily incorporating these intermediary figures into the attributes and status that Israel's God uniquely possessed.

---

111. Philo, *Legat.*115 (my translation), and see further *Legat.*198, 265 on Jewish recalcitrance at worshipping Caligula.

112. Philo, *Legat.* 278 (my translation).

113. Philo, *Legat.* 118. See also Trypho according to Justin Martyr (*Dial.* 68 [Coxe, *ANF*]): "You endeavor to prove an incredible and well-nigh impossible thing; [namely], that God endured to be born and become man."

114. Dunn, *Christology in the Making*, 18.

115. Philo, *Legat.* 6; *Somn.* 1.227–29.

First, it is not entirely clear that the veneration of angels intruded upon reverence for Yahweh or that angels shared in the superlative power and majesty normally assigned to Yahweh. Things are hazy here. The Angel of the Lord is notoriously complex as to who he is and how he relates to Yahweh. While some authors could envisage angels as a projection of God,[116] others mostly regarded such heavenly agents as distinct from God and inferior to God as created beings. According to John Collins: "These texts always distinguish clearly between the supreme God and his angelic lieutenant."[117] A good example of that is the Qumran War Scroll where both the Prince of Light and Belial are inferior to God in terms of power and salvation, leading to the question: "What angel or prince is like you?"[118] In the case of texts and artifacts that point to angel veneration where angelic beings receive prayers for intervention, admiration for their heavenly worship, and thanksgiving for their functions performed on God's behalf, these are not strictly instances of angels receiving divine worship. Rather, as Loren Stuckenbruck concludes after his study of the matter:

> Therefore, on the basis of the texts it would be hasty for one to speak of *the* veneration of angels in Early Judaism. The relevant sources do not allow us to infer a common practice, but rather seem to reflect *specific* contexts within which worship of angels, in a variety of forms, could find expression . . . Angel veneration is not conceived as a substitute for the worship of God. Indeed, most often the venerative language is followed by an explanation which emphasizes the supremacy of God.[119]

116. Justin Martyr, *Dial.* 128.3 (Coxe, *ANF*), claimed that some Jews regarded the Angel of the Lord as "indivisible and inseparable from the Father, just as they say that the light of the sun on earth is indivisible and inseparable from the sun in the heavens . . . so the Father, when He chooses, say they, causes his power to spring forth, and when He chooses, He makes it return to Himself. In this way, they teach, he made the angels."

117. John J. Collins, "Jewish Monotheism and Christian Theology," in *Aspects of Monotheism: How God is One*, ed. Hershel Shanks and Jack Meinhardt (Washington, DC: Biblical Archaeology Society, 1997), 81–105.

118. 1QM 13.10–17.

119. Loren T. Stuckenbruck, *Angel Veneration and Christology: A Study in Early Judaism and in the Christology of the Apocalypse*, WUNT 2.70 (Tübingen: Mohr Siebeck, 1995), 201 (italics original).

Second, exalted human figures never seem to be exalted quite to the same level as Yahweh. The devotion given to Adam by angels in the Life of Adam and Eve 12–16 does not raise "very serious problems for Jewish monotheism"[120] if we consider that within Gen 1 humanity was created to be revered as divinely appointed priest-kings on earth who rule on God's behalf—the real meaning of *imago dei*—while remaining subject to God in both rank and nature. In the story, the Devil baulks at worshipping Adam because he knows that Adam is a created being rather than a heavenly one ("I am prior to him in creation . . . He ought to worship me"). Furthermore, Adam's veneration is at the expense of the Devil's own glory and it is the Devil not Adam who aspires to heavenly grandeur ("a throne above the stars and to be like Most High"). Similarly, while the Enochic Son of Man—who might be Enoch's heavenly doppelgänger—is installed on God's throne and receives obeisance from the kings and rulers of the earth,[121] this is no more than "the eschatological acknowledgement of this figure as God's appointed one who will gather the elect and subdue haughty kings and nations."[122] Even when Moses is heralded as a "God" by Jewish authors like Philo we are not supposed to think that he has incurred into Yahweh's unique position and power, only that he has superlative status and saving power in relation to other human beings.[123] Humans could be exalted to a heavenly station, be equal to the angels, and have Godlike power in relation to other humans, but they did not become equal in majesty and might to Israel's God.

Overall, angelic creatures and exalted human figures were not treated as recipients of cultic worship on the same level of Yahweh in Jewish circles. Jewish devotion showed a concern to preserve God's uniqueness. In their cultic worship they maintained an almost paranoid anxiety about exclusivity. The upshot is that Jewish practice was very

---

120. Contra Chester, *Messiah and Exaltation*, 115.

121. 1 En. 48.5, 62.1–9.

122. Hurtado, *Lord Jesus Christ*, 38.

123. Cf. Philo, *Mos.* 1.158. To illustrate the relational aspect of a human agent acclaimed as a god, in Plautus's *Asinaria* there is a scene where the slave Libanus has acquired the money so that his master Argyrippus can buy his sweetheart Philaenium. But before handing over the money, Libanus relishes the opportunity to taunt his master, commanding him to sacrifice to him (Plautus, *Asinaria* 712–13).

concerned with safeguarding monolatry, suggesting a genuinely robust commitment to a strict monotheism. In which case, devotion to Jesus Christ—not as a second god or an angel beside God but as an expression of faith in the *one* God—is strikingly unusual.[124] The best way to understand these intermediary figures is by adopting the taxonomy proposed by Bauckham and countenancing some of the caveats made by Tilling. These intermediary figures were not ambiguous semi-divine beings spliced with creaturely traits. Some were aspects of God's own unique reality (Logos, Word, Wisdom), while most others were unambiguously creatures, exalted servants by all accounts, but still distinct from God's person, God's sovereignty, and God's worship (e.g., angels, exalted patriarchs, etc.).[125]

The Gospel of Mark is undoubtedly part of this matrix of Jewish monotheism. The Shema of Deut 6:4–6 is affirmed (Mark 12:28–34), God alone can forgive sins (Mark 2:7), God alone is good (Mark 10:18), and God the Father alone knows the timing of Jerusalem's destruction (Mark 13:32). The Markan Jesus himself is a monotheist who proclaims the "gospel of God" and the "kingdom of God" (Mark 1:14–15), he upholds the "commands of God" against Pharisaic halakhah (Mark 7:8–13), he identifies his mission with the will of God (Mark 8:33), he tells people to have faith in God (Mark 11:22), he affirms that God is creator and the God of the patriarchs (Mark 10:1–9; 10:26–27; 13:19), he debates with Herodians about what God deserves to receive (Mark 12:17), and he prays to God (Mark 1:35; 14:32; 15:34). In which case, Mark's conception of divinity is absolutized and inelastic to the point that he "does not and cannot have a general category 'divine' in to which God and other divine beings (Christ, angels) can be placed."[126] How the Markan Jesus relates to God's action and identity is something we will explore soon. For now we can note that Mark, as the Jewish monotheist he was, would find it singularly difficult to imagine a human being elevated to divine status and power.

124. Hurtado, *Lord Jesus Christ*, 31–50.

125. Bauckham, *Jesus and the God of Israel*, 3, 13–17; Tilling, *Paul's Divine Christology*, 61–62.

126. M. Eugene Boring, "Markan Christology: God-Language for Jesus?" *NTS* 45 (1999): 456–57.

Christian Responses to Imperial Deifications

Early comparisons were made between deified figures and the Jesus story. Christian critiques of deification practices presuppose these similarities, seek to explain them, and then mount criticism against the notion of deification itself, at least the pagan sense of deification. Justin Martyr and Origen were fully aware of the similarities between the Jesus story and tales of Herakles or Aesclepius, and the deification of emperors, but they regarded the ancient myths as demonic imitations, and they claimed that deification was not for the wicked but only for the holy and virtuous.[127] The case of Antinous was a particular point of comparison with Jesus since Antinous became a type of religious rival to Christ. Antinous of Bithynia (ca. 111–130 CE) was the teenage lover of the emperor Hadrian, who died along the Nile river in Egypt, and Hadrian had both a temple and a cult established in Antinous's honor.[128] Justin uses the example of Antinous's deification as a prime example of the scandal and silliness of deification, since Antinous was worshiped by imperial fiat and from fear of persecution, even though everyone knew who he was and his origins.[129] Origen mentions Antinous too. Whereas the pagan critic Celsus alleges that the devotion given to Antinous exceeds what the Christians give to Christ, Origen retorts that there is no real comparison between the two as Christ exceeds Antinous in every respect.[130] Others were clearer that Jesus was not divine in the same sense of humans who had been elevated to divine rank. Cyril of Alexandria said: "For there are many anointed ones by grace, who have attained the rank of adoption [as sons], but [there is] only one who is by nature the Son of God."[131] Similar was John Chrysostom: "Christ did not become god from human advancement—perish the thought . . . [W]e preach not a human made into god,

127. Justin, 1 *Apol.* 21–29; *Dial.* 69; Origen, *Cels.* 3.22–23, 36.
128. Dio Cassius, *Hist.* 69.11.2–4.
129. Justin, 1 *Apol.* 29.
130. Origen, *Cels.* 3.36–38. For Antinous, see Trevor W. Thompson, "Antinoos, The New God: Origen on Miracle and Belief in Third-Century Egypt," in *Glaubwürdig oder Unglaubwürdig: Erzählung und Rezeption wunderbarer Ereignisse in der antiken Welt*, ed. Tobias Nicklas and Janet E. Spittler, WUNT 321 (Mohr Siebeck, 2013), 143–73.
131. Cyril of Alexandria, *Frag.* 190.

but confess a god made human."[132] Minucius Felix claimed "Miserable indeed" are those whose hope is a "mortal man" like princes and kings for "to invoke their deity" and to worship them with sacrifices is "a false flattery."[133] Even the second-century critic Celsus—who was far from hesitant at pointing out the similarities between pagan mythologies and the Gospels—could deny that gods or sons of the gods became human. He wrote: "O Jews and Christians, no God or Son of God either came or will come down [to earth]. But if you mean that angels did so, then what do you call them? Are they gods, or some other race of beings? Some other race of beings [doubtlessly], and in all probability daemons."[134] Celsus did not think that pagan mythologies provided a precedent for Christian views about Jesus. He really struggles to understand precisely what kind of divine visitation Christians thought happened in the coming of Jesus. Finally, it is worth mentioning that Jesus, unlike deified heroes and emperors, was never worshiped in his own cult independent of God the Father. He was not given his own shrine next to Yahweh like Augustus was slotted next to Roma or Jupiter. Worship of the Father could no longer be independent of Jesus. However, worship of Jesus necessarily involved worship of God the Father. Christians never regarded any divinized human figures as examples of their beliefs about Jesus, but saw in them only pale imitations of the Jesus story.

Conclusion

In this section we have explored whether Mark's Jesus story was modelled on the Hellenistic trope of humans becoming divine. A negative verdict was given in light of several things: Greco-Roman critiques of divinization meant that it was a contestable process rather than an incontestable norm; Jewish monotheism, which Mark shares, was strict enough to rule out enrolling human figures into a heavenly pantheon; and Christian authors took time to rebuff claims that Jesus was a human figure who was

---

132. John Chrysostom, *PG* 61.697, 38–42, cited in in Litwa, *Ieus Deus*, 2.
133. Minucius Felix, *Oct.* 29 (Wallis, *ANF* [amended]).
134. Origen, *Cels.* 5.2 (Crombie, *ANF*).

deified, not denying the similarities, but highlighting the differences with the deification process. What remains to be done in the next chapter is to examine whether Mark has a backwards movement of Christology and whether Mark thinks that Jesus became the Son of God at his baptism.

CHAPTER 4

The Gospel of Mark and the Son of God

As demonstrated in the previous chapter, the deification of humans was a contested practice in the Greco-Roman world. Although bestowing divine honors on rulers was widespread and the deification of emperors and their family members was established by precedent, a number of philosophers rejected the idea in principle and others mocked the character of those deified as unworthy of divine honors. In addition, the deification of humans was generally incompatible with both the monotheism of Second Temple Judaism and the monotheism expressed in early Christian writings. That implies that Mark's Gospel, with its strong monotheistic emphasis, is unlikely to envisage Jesus as a deified figure. Be that as it may, many have suggested that adoptionism, at least in part, explains much of Mark's presentation of Jesus, where Jesus is presented as a human figure who is adopted to divine sonship. This chapter will engage in a close reading of Mark's Gospel in order to (1) contend against an adoptionist reading of the Markan story and (2) establish that Mark's Christology as a whole exhibits a form of christological monotheism where Jesus is part of the divine identity.

The Markan Baptism Scene

The opening section of Mark's Gospel is bracketed with the incipit at one end that describes the "beginning of the gospel of Jesus Christ" (Mark 1:1) and at the other end with the description of Jesus himself preaching the "gospel of God" and the "kingdom of God" at the commencement of his Galilean ministry (Mark 1:14–15). Sandwiched in between is the ministry of John the Baptist (Mark 1:2–8), the baptism of Jesus (Mark 1:9–11), and Jesus's temptation in the wilderness (Mark 1:12–13). The baptism is crucial because it features Jesus's debut in the Markan story. More specifically, it presents Jesus as a faithful Israelite who is baptized by John. The accompanying portents of a heavenly voice and the vision of a dove descending from heaven indicate, at the least, a revelation of divine approval with Jesus presenting himself for baptism. But an approval unto what?

Καὶ ἐγένετο ἐν ἐκείναις ταῖς ἡμέραις ἦλθεν Ἰησοῦς ἀπὸ Ναζαρὲτ τῆς Γαλιλαίας καὶ ἐβαπτίσθη εἰς τὸν Ἰορδάνην ὑπὸ Ἰωάννου. καὶ εὐθὺς ἀναβαίνων ἐκ τοῦ ὕδατος εἶδεν σχιζομένους τοὺς οὐρανοὺς καὶ τὸ πνεῦμα ὡς περιστερὰν καταβαῖνον εἰς αὐτόν· καὶ φωνὴ ἐγένετο ἐκ τῶν οὐρανῶν· σὺ εἶ ὁ υἱός μου ὁ ἀγαπητός, ἐν σοὶ εὐδόκησα.

And it happened in those days, Jesus came from Nazareth of Galilee and was baptized in the Jordan by John. And immediately as he was rising up out of the water, he saw the heavens being torn open and the Spirit descending on him like a dove. And a voice came from the heavens, "You are my Son, the Beloved; with you I am well pleased." (Mark 1:9–11)

According to Dunn, "Whether Mark intended it or not, his treatment at this point left his account open to the interpretation that Jesus first *became* the Son of God at the beginning of his ministry, by endowment with the Spirit and divine ratification, and Mark evidently took no pains to rule out such an interpretation."[1] The baptism by itself, when unhinged from its wider narrative context, certainly can lend itself to such a reading. Perhaps all the more so if subsequent readers of Mark's Gospel were immersed in the tradition of Greek and Roman gods begetting progeny on earth and the traditions of Roman emperors adopting heirs into the imperial family and so making them, sooner or later, sons of the deified emperor.

1. Dunn, *Christology in the Making*, 47 (italics original).

Michael Peppard and The Son of God in the Roman World

Peppard's erudite volume *The Son of God in the Roman World* critiques theological readings—i.e., explicitly Nicene accounts—of first-century texts, while also seeking to interpret divine sonship in the socio-political context of the Roman Empire.[2] Peppard reads the Gospel of Mark, especially the baptism episode, in light of Roman adoption practices and the imperial cults. His conclusion is:

> Reading the baptism of Jesus through the lens of imperial ideology encourages one to hear the divine voice as an adoption, the beginning of Jesus' accession as son and heir. The dove functions as an omen of his grace and counter-symbol to the eagle, which was a public portent of divine favor and election in Roman culture. . . . Viewed in its Roman socio-political context, Mark's Christology was as high as humanly possible. When facing the novel challenge of narrating the divine sonship of a human being—in relation to a God that did not procreate—Mark crafted a portrayal that was theologically coherent and also resonated in its cultural context. The resurrected metaphor enables us to read Mark anew.[3]

By adoption, he means a device whereby "Mark narratively characterized Jesus in comparison with the adopted Roman emperor, the most powerful man-god in the universe."[4]

Of course, accepting Peppard's thesis requires moving the cerebral furniture around one's mental construction of early Christology and deleting the Nicene default setting. Hengel once asserted that the title *divi filius*/Θεοῦ υἱός in the imperial cult was not "a serious influence on the conceptuality of the early Christianity that was developing in Palestine and Syria" and this "official, secular state religion was at best a negative

---

2. Peppard's book, *Son of God*, has probably influenced Kirk, *A Man Attested by God*, 210, since Kirk supposes that the Markan Jesus is "the adopted, messianic son of God, specially chosen to represent God's reign to the world and to take his throne along the way of rejection, death, and suffering."

3. Peppard, *Son of God*, 5.

4. Peppard, *Son of God*, 95.

stimulus, not a model [for christological development]."[5] In contrast, Peppard's suggestion is that the imperial cult and Roman adoptive practices were a major influence on the formation of early presentations of Jesus, with Mark becoming the case in point.

Peppard's work is commendable for a number of reasons. First, Peppard is drawing on a far more accurate and nuanced understanding of the Roman imperial cults than previous generations, which wrote them off as little more than political propaganda in a religious veil. More recent studies have shown that the imperial cults were religiously quite meaningful for their participants as they were part of an empire-wide network of patron-client relationships where benefaction was reciprocated with divine worship. Second, Peppard presents a thorough and convincing description of ancient adoption practices and their meaning among Roman elites. Third, he provides an interesting account of the interface of adoptive and begotten imagery in the early patristic period. Fourth, and best of all, Peppard provides insights into how the christological claims of Mark's Gospel might have resonated among those immersed in Greco-Roman culture where the imperial cults were extant and where adoption was practiced. To distill that further, Peppard has demonstrated that it is certainly possible to read Mark's baptismal story, on its own, as a story of a human being adopted as God's Son. And further, this would not necessarily be perceived as a low evaluation of Jesus in the minds of audiences because Jesus had been graciously adopted as the divine Son, hailed as a counter-emperor no less, and reached the highest point that any human could possibly ever attain.

That said, I do have several points of query and criticism against Peppard's overall case:

(1) Peppard's critique of the Nicene readings as focused heavily on ontological matters strikes me as unfair.

Yes, the Nicenes and post-Nicenes drank long and deep at the pool of middle Platonism. This undoubtedly shaped their construction of Christology, often setting them adrift from the world inside the New Testament that was less sophistic and speculative about the nature of divinity. However, abstract reflections on the nature of gods did not begin with

---

5. Hengel, *Son of God*, 30, see similarly Hurtado, *Lord Jesus Christ*, 92–99.

Cyril of Alexandria or the Cappadocian Fathers. These ideas had a long history in the Greco-Roman world. Socrates discoursed on whether the gods, being immortal, incorporeal, and immutable, were able to rule over mortal beings.[6] The language of deities as "eternal and unbegotten" (ἀΐδιοι καὶ ἀγεννήτοι) did not originate in Christian theism, but found mention in Plutarch's discussion of the god Apollo in contrast to deified mortals.[7] As we have seen, the ontological distinction between the eternal and imperishable gods and finite humans was at the heart of Philo's critique of Caligula's claims to divine status.[8] Furthermore, why must we assume that the ideas expressed in Cicero's *On the Nature of Gods*, with its dialogues about different conceptions of deity, was far removed from popular devotion of the pious folk who practiced cultic worship? Why believe that such folks were so fixated on the daily struggle for survival that they were completely disinterested in anything approaching "theology"?[9] True enough, practitioners of Roman religion wanted plentiful harvests and deliverance from disease. They likely did not pontificate as to whether Jupiter was the same god as Serapis while the city was ravaged with plague or when Alemannic hordes threatened to pour down the Rhineland into northern Italy. Yet someone observing imperial cultic rituals could conceivably ask, "Does giving divine honors equal to that of Jupiter to a dead man mean that the dead man is himself equal to Jupiter?" or "What actually happens at deification?" Viewed this way, getting your head around the notion of deification is not a problem merely for those with a Christianized conception of monotheism, but proved to be just as puzzling to the Romans too.[10]

If common people found time to discuss politics in the fields or in a tavern, then they found time to talk about religion, for imperial powers and prerogatives of the deities were intertwined. Along this line, scholars should have noticed that Paul, the Jewish tentmaker from Tarsus, could write to various Christian congregations, comprised of diverse social ranks ranging from aediles to slaves, about the specific nature of Israel's God and even that of the pagan gods. In which case, Paul's terse

6. Plato, *Phaedo*, 98–99.
7. Plutarch, *Pel.* 16.5.
8. Philo, *Legat.* 93–118, 278.
9. Gradel, *Emperor Worship and Roman Religion*, 3; Peppard, *Son of God*, 33.
10. Beard, North, Price, *Religions of Rome*, 1:148.

remarks about the nature of divinity are not remarkable. Rather, they are part of an inherited Jewish and Greco-Roman tradition that imagined something of the nature of deities and daemons (see Gal 4:8; 1 Cor 8:4; 10:20–21). Paul's description of Christ as one who was in the "image of God" (2 Cor 4:4; Col 1:15), the "form of God" (Phil 2:6; cf. Philo, *Legat.* 110), embodying the "fullness of deity in bodily form" (Col 2:9), also implies a certain ontology within Jesus's relationship to God the Father. Paul used this language of divine being and divine form with the reasonable assumption that readers knew something of it and were genuinely interested in the subject of the nature of the gods. Peppard wisely admits that a divine ontology could emerge over time. He notes: "When continuous benefactions led to continuous honors, that process could admittedly lead to a kind of ontology—a status solidified because of a god's perpetual benefactions."[11] I would press this further and contend that ontology is a function of worldview, for all worldviews that have conceptions of cosmology and divinity operate with a tacit ontology, whether openly acknowledged or not, and assume some type of reality undergirding religious devotion. While the average Marcus or Livia worshipping in the temples of Rome were not platonic philosophers, we should not be forced into a dichotomy of religion as purely "cultic devotion" or religion as "philosophical speculation." Rather, ritual expressed ontology and ontology informed ritual.[12]

In addition, whereas Peppard thinks that abstract ontological reflection led to the unfair rejection of the adoptive metaphor of sonship, I would aver that the shoe is on the other foot. It was proponents of adoptionist Christologies who were largely driven by ontological concerns in pressing for adoptionism. If one starts with the premise of divine unity, divine simplicity, and divine immutability—common notions in early Greco-Roman philosophy—then God's being can have no becoming, because if a god

---

11. Peppard, *Son of God*, 35.

12. Note the words of Michael Frede, "The Case for Pagan Monotheism," in *One God: Pagan Monotheism in the Roman Empire*, ed. Stephen Mitchell and Peter van Nuffelen (Cambridge: Cambridge University Press, 2010), 81: "In conclusion I want to say that ancient religion is not just a matter of cult and ritual, but that ancient religious thought and writing are a crucial part of it, especially if these themselves are regarded as religious activities."

can change, then he or she is not fully god. This was one way of showing that the supreme God was better than the anthropomorphic gods of the pantheon who swoop down to earth for mischief or leisure.[13] So if Jesus changes from one location to another, whether from heaven to earth or from earth to heaven, then he cannot be divine in an absolute sense. The result of such an ontological presupposition is that one would naturally pursue interpretations of Jesus's sonship that are necessarily subordinationist and ontologically inferior to the Father. So, "Yeah, of course Jesus is divine, but not divine like the Most High God is divine! That God does not and cannot change, and his chariot does not swing this low." If one operates in that ontological scheme, then a subordinationist Christology will prove to be a logical necessity, with Jesus as a lesser divine being than the supremely divine Father who is both impassible and immutable.[14] And the most convenient place to back up your subordinationist Christology is with a strict reliance on the Synoptic narratives in tandem with a conception of divine sonship that majors on something like adoption.[15]

Finally, the claims made about Jesus by the church fathers were not merely the imposition of a platonic ontology or the attempt to run roughshod over socio-political images for sonship. More likely, Nicene Christology was the attempt to demonstrate the parity of a particular grammar of divine ontology with the christological narratives of Scripture. For case in point, *homoousios* is simply deploying ontological language to express

---

13. See Cicero, *Nat. d.* 1.29.

14. According to Collins, "Jewish Monotheism and Christian Theology," 102: "The notion that there was a second divine being *under* God was not intrinsically incompatible with Judaism, although the belief that Jesus of Nazareth was such a being seemed preposterous to many Jews. What was incompatible with Judaism was the idea that this second divine being was equal to God" (italics original). Similarly, Oskar Skarsaune, "Is Christianity Monotheistic? Patristic Perspectives on a Jewish/Christian Debate," *Studia Patristica* 29 (1997): 362, notes: "Seen from a Jewish perspective the Christians were doing one of two things. Either they deified a man of purely human origin—which was blasphemy plain and simple. Or, if the Christian claims about Jesus were true, that he was divine from the beginning, Christology raised the whole question of divine suffering, the suffering of God."

15. One could make the case that what drove some "heterodox" christological readings of the Gospels was an *a priori* commitment to divine impassibility, which is why several writings depict the divine Christ leaving the man Jesus just prior to his crucifixion (see Irenaeus, *Haer.* 1.8.2; 1.24.4; Disc. Seth 56.6–13; Apoc. Pet. 81.6–23, 82.1–3).

what Paul and John affirm in their own way: Jesus is equal with God (see Phil 2:5 and John 5:18).[16] Nicene Christology was the attempt to exposit the New Testament's claims about Jesus by utilizing the philosophical tools that were on hand. It was a deliberate theological reading informed by philosophy, but it was not therefore pure anachronism or mere allegory.[17]

(2) Peppard does not deny the presence of scriptural allusions in Mark's baptismal story, but he deliberately downplays their prominence.[18] This is probably the weakest part of his otherwise commendable thesis. The problem is, as Richard Hays notes, many of the key images for Jesus in the Markan narrative are drawn from Israel's Scriptures. "Indeed," Hays writes, "a reader who fails to discern the significance of these images can hardly grasp Mark's message."[19] The Markan Jesus is

16. The language of "equal with God" (Phil 2:5; John 5:18) could be regarded as honorific rather than ontological. Yet, in the case of Phil 2:5–11 and the wider sway of the Gospel of John we find evidence that ontological grammar is never far away. In Philippians, the reference to Jesus being the "form of God" (Phil 2:6–7) who takes on "humanity" speaks to his pre-incarnate divine nature. Similarly, the Johannine language of Father and Son interpenetrating one another entails that their relationship is grounded in something ontological (John 10:38; 14:10–12, 20; 17:21).

17. Christopher Bryan, *The Resurrection of the Messiah* (Oxford: Oxford University Press, 2011), 178, writes: "Catholic Christianity has claimed that by the *homoousion* of the Niceno-Constantinopolitan formularies it elucidated what the New Testament already implied." Boring, "Markan Christology," 471, states: "The explicit use of God-language for Jesus by later NT authors and the classical creeds is in continuity with the Christology already present in Mark. To state the matter somewhat provocatively: John, Nicea, and Chalcedon understood and developed Mark's Christology in a more profound sense than was done by either Matthew or Luke. Chalcedon may perhaps be understood as more 'Markan' than 'Johannine,' since John has more explicit subordinationist tendencies than does Mark. Christians who are concerned with both canon and creed need not therefore attempt to get Mark to be Nicean or Johannine, but should attempt to understand Mark in his own terms." See also David S. Yeago, "The New Testament and Nicene Dogma: A Contribution to the Recovery of Theological Exegesis," in *Theological Interpretation of Scripture: Classic and Contemporary Readings*, ed. Stephen E. Fowl (Malden, MA: Blackwell, 1997), 87–100, who helpfully distinguishes "judgments" as material claims one detects in a text, while "concepts" are the contingent forms that one uses to explain those judgments.

18. Peppard, *Son of God*, 86, 94. A similar complaint is lodged by Bates, *Birth of the Trinity*, 78n72.

19. Richard B. Hays, *Reading Backwards: Figural Christology and the Fourfold Gospel Witness* (Waco, TX: Baylor University Press, 2014), 17.

so interwoven with scriptural imagery that either glossing over it or mis-representing Mark's intertextuality is going to lead to a skewed view of Mark's Christology.

Even so, on the baptism of Jesus, Peppard maintains that the presence of allusions to Ps 2:7 and Isa 42:1 are not "unshakable." He thinks instead that Roman adoption practices are a better matrix for understanding the episode.[20] The problem is, by any criteria, we have clear scriptural allusions in the Markan baptismal story, especially when we view these allusions as part of a wider pattern of scriptural citations, allusions, and echoes across Mark's Gospel as a whole. To be precise, in Mark 1:11, we have a clear allusion to Ps 2:7 about the enthronement of Israel's king as Yahweh's "son," a very probable allusion to Isa 42:1 about the anointing of the Servant who receives the Spirit and in whom Yahweh delights, and a possible echo of Akedah tradition in Gen 22:2, 12, 16 about Abraham's willingness to offer up his beloved son, Isaac.[21] The voice from heaven then blends together a trio of scriptural images about the Davidic king, Isaiah's Servant, and the Akedah to reveal Jesus as a redemptive figure who will effect Israel's restoration through the power bestowed on him through the Holy Spirit. The king is elected as son, the Isaianic servant is anointed for his service, and Abraham's beloved son is readied for sacrifice. It is certainly possible that the baptism of Jesus may not have meant for Mark what it meant for later proto-orthodox and orthodox interpreters. Yet it seems evident to me that the intertextual allusions point to the call and commission of Jesus as the Son and Servant to complete his messianic task; it marks him out as the *messias designatus*, not as one who becomes the divine Son at this juncture. Moreover, Sam Janse's superb study of the reception history of Ps 2 has shown that this text provides the

---

20. Peppard, *Son of God*, 95–96.

21. On the difference between types of citation, allusion, and echo, see Stanley E. Porter, "Further Comments on the Use of the Old Testament in the New Testament," in *The Intertextuality of the Epistles: Explorations in Theory and Practice*, ed. Thomas L. Brodie, Dennis R. MacDonald, and Stanley E. Porter, NTM 16 (Sheffield: Sheffield Phoe-nix, 2007), 107–9. For commentary on the texts alluded to and echoed in Mark 1:11, see Thomas R. Hatina, "Embedded Scripture Texts and the Plurality of Meaning: The Announcement of the 'Voice from Heaven' in Mark 1.11 as a Case Study," in *Biblical Interpretation in Early Christian Gospels: Volume 1—The Gospel of Mark*, ed. Thomas R. Hatina, LNTS 304 (London: T&T Clark, 2006), 81–99.

"backbone" of Mark's Gospel with the emphasis on the enthronement of Jesus as King.[22] If the choice is whether Mark's christological narration in the baptism scene is determined by scriptural allusions or by an assumed background in Roman adoption practices, our preference should unreservedly be for the former.

(3) Peppard believes that understanding ancient adoption practices, especially adoption into the imperial family, can illuminate how early readers might have resonated with Mark's baptism story and the Gospel as a whole.[23] This has some traction in wider scholarship. For instance,

22. Sam Janse, *"You Are My Son": The Reception History of Psalm 2 in Early Judaism and the Early Church* (Leuven: Peeters, 2009), 158; see similarly Joel Marcus, *The Way of the Lord: Christological Exegesis of the Old Testament in the Gospel of Mark* (Louisville: Westminster John Knox, 1992), 68–69. Psalm 2 is the second most quoted and alluded to text from the Old Testament in the New Testament, Ps 110 being the most prevalent. Psalm 2 is most likely a pre-exilic enthronement Psalm, showing signs of Egyptian influence, celebrating the ritualized enthronement of Israel's king, and climaxing in the king being celebrated as Yahweh's "son." There is no question of Ps 2 portraying the king as an incarnation or manifestation of Yahweh as was common in Egyptian and Assyrian tradition. Israelite tradition insisted on a divide between humans and Yahweh. The fact that the Israelite king is "begotten" at a precise point, "today," underscores the metaphorical nature of the begetting, thus the king is not the product of a sexual union between Yahweh and any consort. Even describing the declaration as an "adoption" might not be precise. (1) Adoption does not figure in Israelite royal ideology. (2) In the Psalms specifically and in the Old Testament more generally, the king remains distinct from Yahweh. He is not a member of a heavenly court. There is no claim for epiphanic greatness. He is primarily an earthly vassal of Yahweh even if Yahweh has chosen him to rule over the nations on his behalf. (3) The application of divine titles to Israel's king were sparse (see Ps 45:6; Isa 9:6). The king was never made the object of cultic veneration, which makes sense if divine sonship is fictive rather than filial. (4) The sonship language most likely implies office and status with the imperative that the king must imitate Yahweh in ruling over the people and judging in righteousness (see Ps 89:27). (5) Given that Israel was metaphorically a nation of divine sons (Exod 4:22; Hos 11:1) and given the king's role as mirroring the people to Yahweh, the king is perhaps best described as "elected" rather than "adopted" precisely because he shares in the national identity of divine sonship; indeed, he is the representative of it before Yahweh. In which case, as Collins and Collins, *King and Messiah as Son of God*, 22, put it, "The main implication of the declaration that the king was son of God is the implication that he is empowered to act as God's surrogate on earth."

23. Peppard, *Son of God*, 6, 26–28. Adela Y. Collins, *Mark*, Hermeneia (Minneapolis: Fortress, 2007), 150, while rejecting the adoptionist reading, notes this as a possibility: "Yet it may be that this language evoked ideas of adoption in at least some of the

Talbert writes: "The issue of Jesus' status may ultimately have depended on the Christians who employed the model. If a former pagan heard the model in terms of the myth of the demi-gods, then that one may have thought of Jesus as an immortal."[24] Adela Collins makes a similar point: even while early Christianity was rooted in religious experiences and Jewish traditions, she believes that the "prior cultural experiences" and the "cultural situation" of Christians in the Greco-Roman world played a significant role in shaping and interpreting christological beliefs.[25] Given the presence of Greco-Roman culture and religion in Palestine—including the imperial cult at Caesarea Maritima, Caesarea-Philippi, and Sebaste-Samaria[26]—Collins asserts that we "should take seriously the likelihood that non-Jewish Hellenistic and Roman traditions, as well as Jewish traditions, shaped the religious experiences, ideas and writings of especially the Greek-speaking Jewish followers of Jesus in the period immediately following his death." She further finds it plausible that such traditions were "deliberately and consciously" adapted in order to construct a meaningful system of belief.[27] In the end, readers confronted with the phrase, "Jesus the Son of God," would think differently about it depending on if they were Jews, Greeks, or Romans.[28] Reading is a matter of context. If a pagan reader immersed in Greco-Roman literature about Herakles and Dionysus, adoptive practices, and public rituals for the deification of emperors were to read Mark 1:9–11, she or he might well think that Jesus was adopted as God's Son. It could very well "mean" that to such a person.

---

early social contexts in which Mark was read and heard." See also Whitenton, *Kyriotic Sonship*, 140.

24. Talbert, "The Development of Christology," 12.

25. Adela Y. Collins, "The Worship of Jesus and the Imperial Cult," in *The Jewish Roots of Christological Monotheism: Papers from the St. Andrews Conference on the Historical Origins of the Worship of Jesus*, ed. Carey C. Newman, James R. Davila, and Gladys S. Lewis, JSJSup 63 (Leiden: Brill, 1999), 235, 241.

26. See Josephus, *A.J.* 15.339; *B.J.* 1.414 (Caesarea Maritima), *A.J.* 15.298 (Sebaste), and *A.J.* 15.363–64; *B.J.* 1.404–6 (Panion/Omrit near Caesarea-Philippi).

27. Collins, "The Worship of Jesus and the Imperial Cult," 242.

28. Adela Yarbro Collins, "Mark and His Readers: The Son of God among Jews," *HTR* 92 (1999): 393–408; Adela Yarbro Collins, "Mark and His Readers: The Son of God among Greeks and Romans," *HTR* 93 (2000): 85–100; and similarly Whitenton, *Hearing Kyriotic Sonship*, 137–40.

What is more, we have proof that Mark could be, and was, read in light of divergent christological systems in the second century, some of them constructed in such a way as to make adoptionism a natural choice given their theology, anthropology, and cosmology.[29]

However, readers can be naïve and contexts are infinite. We have to find a way to adjudicate between different reader responses, especially if one is interested in pursuing a reading that seeks to be both coherent and normative for the symbolic world of the first Christians. I would suggest that what legitimates textual meaning is not how a text might resonate with any one person based on his or her own personal experiences and contexts. Such readings can be multiplied endlessly. Imagine a Jehovah's Witness from New York, an atheist from Portland, a Buddhist from Thailand, or a Hindu from Bali reading Mark 1:9–11 for the first time. The possible resonances of the text with their indigenous religious cultures would be manifold![30] Rather than treat all textual resonances as self-authenticating, I think what makes an interpretation preferable is that it creates a web of connections between the author, the text, and readers that is able to hold together all the multiplicity of factors in the reading process. So the question is not, could some Roman Dickianus or Greek Honarios look at the Gospel of Mark and say, "Hey, that reminds me of Vespasian's consecration as a god and Nerva's adoption of Trajan." The question is, what reading best explains the author's intention, the dynamics inside the text, the intended response for the implied reader,

---

29. Michael J. Kok, *The Gospel on the Margins: The Reception of Mark in the Second Century* (Minneapolis: Fortress, 2015), 244.

30. To give an example, D. A. Carson of Trinity Evangelical Divinity School once told a funny story of a Buddhist monk in Thailand who was given a copy of the four Gospels by an American missionary to read at his leisure. The monk caught up with the missionary a week later and was very excited to discuss the contents with the missionary. "This Jesus is God," the monk said excitedly, "and he's even greater than Buddha!" At this point the American missionary was encouraged and thought this conversion story would be a gem for his monthly newsletter home. The American then asked the Buddhist monk to explain why he thought Jesus was greater than Buddha. "Well," replied the monk, "Jesus is born, and then he dies. Jesus is born and then he dies again. Jesus is born and then he dies yet again. Jesus is born, he dies, except this time he's called 'god.' It took Jesus only four lifetimes to become god; it took the Buddha over a thousand." The monk was reading the four Gospels as four consecutive incarnations of Jesus's lifetime.

and the experiences of real readers that we encounter in reception history? A preferential reading is one that can hold together all those factors with a firm coherence over and against alternative proposals. Peppard enters into this enterprise of adjudicating between conflicting readings by contending as he does that Mark's Christology "ought" to be understood independently of (though not necessarily adverse to) later high Christologies and Nicene cosmologies.[31] My counter-claim is that Mark's purpose, text, and reception history is such that Greco-Roman adoption practices and the imperial cult are in some cases a useful analogue, but ought not to be regarded as a hermeneutical key for unlocking Mark's christological door.

Mark's Non-Adoptionist Baptism Story

I hasten to add that there are several good reasons for doubting the utility of Roman adoption practices as the background for understanding the Markan baptismal account. Following Philip Davis, I regard the interpretation of the baptismal scene in an adoptionist way as "untenable" for several reasons.[32]

For a start, if Jesus's adoption was the reward for his previous deportment, then one wonders why Mark never mentions the meritorious

---

31. Peppard, Son of God, 6–7.

32. Philip G. Davis, "Mark's Christological Paradox," in The Synoptic Gospels: A Sheffield Reader, ed. Craig A. Evans and Stanley E. Porter (Sheffield: Sheffield Academic Press, 1995), 174–75. See also David E. Garland, A Theology of Mark's Gospel, BTNT (Grand Rapids: Zondervan, 2015), 218–20. Note too the comments of M. Eugene Boring, Mark: A Commentary (Louisville: Westminster John Knox, 2006), 46: "The declaration from heaven should not be misunderstood in an adoptionist sense." Collins, Mark, 150, notes: "The widespread view that the language of Ps 2:7 implies adoption in its original social and historical contexts is not tenable." Also, Paul Owen, "Jesus as God's Chief Agent in Mark's Christology," in Mark, Manuscripts, and Monotheism: Essays in Honor of Larry W. Hurtado, ed. Chris Keith and Dieter T. Roth, LNTS 528 (London: Bloomsbury, 2015), 56: "if the contours of this study are even broadly correct, then it is quite impossible, for example, to argue that in Mark 1:11, Jesus is presented as a normal man who is first adopted and elevated to divine sonship at his baptism."

early life that so warranted divine adoption as its reward. Mark presents Jesus's baptism as the beginning of the gospel, not as the beginning of Jesus.

Following on from that, the voice from heaven announces God's delight in the beloved son and the aorist verb εὐδόκησα is not a simple past ("I was pleased"), nor inceptive ("I have become pleased"), but more properly gnomic, something that is timeless and regularly true (i.e., "At whatever moment one cares to ask, I am pleased").[33] Thus God was always pleased with Jesus, the Son. Grammatically there is no question of him being made the Son.[34]

---

33. Contra Boring, *Mark*, 43, and see Joel Marcus, *Mark 1–8: A New Translation with Introduction and Commentary*, AB (New York: Doubleday, 2000), 162, who takes εὐδόκησα to signify "a past divine choice of Jesus being ratified at his baptism." On the gnomic aorist, see Stanley E. Porter, *Idioms of the Greek New Testament*, 2nd ed. (Sheffield: Sheffield Academic Press, 1992), 38.

34. Peppard, *Son of God*, 106–12, contends that εὐδοκέω in Mark 1:11 is better translated as "pleased to choose." He offers precedents in the LXX and other Greco-Roman examples, including a Roman adoption contract! He thinks the NT usage of εὐδοκέω only rarely connotes to be "pleased," "satisfied," or "to consent" and ordinarily is construed as something like to "choose," "elect," or "decree." If the verb signifies election or choice, then, in conjunction with the punctiliar aspect of the aorist form, it inveighs against understanding εὐδόκησα as a "static approval of a pre-existing condition" (112). Rather, it supports an interpretation of Jesus's baptism as a scene of adoption. Peppard's lexical summary is an important reminder that the semantic range of εὐδοκέω includes "chose" and "elect." Nevertheless, his discussion suffers from two flaws. First, εὐδοκέω does not mean any one thing in English; rather, it belongs to the semantic range of attitudes and emotions that involve a resulting pleasure, for which a mixture of "choose" or "pleased" is often the most fitting English rendering depending on the context (BDAG, 404). It might be more proper to say that in εὐδοκέω all things that one takes pleasure in require choosing to delight in them in the first place. We should surmise that εὐδοκέω cannot be reduced to "to choose" anymore more than to "to please." Second, the aorist verb form does not describe a punctiliar action, depicting a singular one-off event, but is aspectually perfective (i.e., views the action externally) and grammaticalizes a complete and undifferentiated process. See Porter, *Idioms of the Greek New Testament*, 35, and Constantine Campbell, *Basics of Verbal Aspect in Biblical Greek* (Grand Rapids: Zondervan, 2008), 34–39, esp. 36. For an aorist verb to be punctiliar, that would depend on *Aktionsart* (i.e., the pragmatics of aspect) rather than on an action inherent in the verbal form itself. The problem in the case of εὐδόκησα in Mark 1:11 is that a punctiliar *Aktionsart* requires a punctiliar lexeme, which εὐδοκέω is arguably not.

Given the widespread attestation of Jesus's pre-existence in Christian sources contemporary with Mark,[35] Davis is right that "any espousal of adoptionism would need to be quite pointed; but this we do not find."[36] Quite the reverse is apparent: there are telltale signs that Mark has a tacit conception of Jesus's pre-existence *as a divine son*. It should be granted that the baptism story itself leaves the issue of Jesus's pre-existence open or at least ambiguous.[37] Even so, the baptism story is not the final word on the subject. While we can and will say more about Mark's κύριος language for Jesus and what it implies about Jesus's identity, a *prima facie* case for the pre-existence of the Markan Jesus is evidenced by his reception from demons. During one exorcism in a synagogue, a man possessed by an unclean spirit cried out, "What do you want with us, Jesus of Nazareth? Have you come to destroy us? I know who you are—the Holy One of God!" (Mark 1:24). And the narrator later describes Jesus's ministry in Galilee, informing readers that "whenever the unclean spirits saw him, they fell prostrate before him and cried out, 'You are the Son of God.'" The story of Jesus's encounter with the Gerasene demoniac afflicted by a legion of demons includes the demoniac running to Jesus and shouting: "What do you want with me, Jesus, Son of the Most High God? I implore you before God, don't torture me!" (Mark 5:7). It is not simply a question of the demons knowing about Jesus, they know him to be the "Holy One of God" and the "Son

35. Active and personal pre-existence (Phil 2:6–8; 2 Cor 8:9; Heb 2:14, 17); descent from heaven (1 Cor 15:47; Rom 10:6); Jesus as the Lord and Creator (1 Cor 8:6; Col 1:16; Heb 1:2); sending of the son from heaven (Gal 4:4; Rom 8:3); Christ in Israel's history (1 Cor 10:4, 9; Jude 5). See discussion in Gathercole, *Preexistent Son*, 23–45.

36. I would also add that pre-existence, in some form, was attributed to Augustus and claimed by Caligula, so that any Christology constructed in counter-point to imperial ideology might be pressed to also include pre-existence, see Horace, *Carm.* 1.2 (Augustus) and Philo, *Legat.* 56 (Caligula).

37. See R. T. France, *The Gospel of Mark: A Commentary on the Greek Text*, NIGTC (Grand Rapids; Eerdmans, 2002), 74: "Mark here introduces Jesus into his narrative for the first time, we are given no indication of what consciousness, if any, he had before his baptism of either his mission or his unique relationship to God. The question is of interest to us, both for our attempts to write the biography of the historical Jesus and for christological debate. But Mark offers no retrospect from this point. His focus is entirely forward-looking."

of God" who has come from somewhere on the God-side of the heaven-creation divide, and has divine authority to destroy them. This knowledge of Jesus held by the demons was not apprehended by witnessing Jesus's baptism nor ascertained from the demonic rumor mill; rather, the demons know Jesus because they know his origins, his identity, his power, and his purpose, and it literally scares them off the human bones they inhabit. Gathercole rightly concludes: "[T]he recognition of Jesus' identity by the demons is in line with the divine verdict announced at the opening of the Gospel: Jesus' identity in relation to the Father is fully seen in the course of his ministry only by other heavenly figures. As such, he is not merely a temporary visitor to the heavenly council, like the prophets, but rather a *permanent* member."[38] This textual data puts us in a position to contest Peppard's claim: "If Mark was trying to depict Jesus as already God's Son, he did not do a very good job. Maybe that was not his intention."[39]

Finally, according to Davis, Mark's construal of the divine-human dichotomy is "too radical for the implication which arises from adoptionism, which is that the gulf could be bridged from the human side." To fill out Davis's point, Mark presents an epistemological (Mark 4:11–12; 13:32), soteriological (Mark 2:7; 14:25), and ontological (Mark 10:18) dichotomy between God and humanity. Mark's Jesus traverses that divide because as the Son of Man he originates on the divine side of this chasm, which is why he carries the full weight of divine authority (Mark 2:28; 13:26;

---

38. Gathercole, *The Preexistent Son*, 54 (italics original). Contrasted with Kirk, *A Man Attested by God*, 205–9, who declares, "Because the spirits' knowledge includes both the natural, human identity of Jesus and his secret status with respect to God, we cannot conclude from their recognition of him that they are identifying someone whom they know from a pre-existent past." All the demons know "is what the reader knows, and what has been disclosed to Jesus at his baptism: that he is the son of God" (206). The problem is that the spirits were not mentioned at his baptism nor do they mention his baptism. As far as we can tell, they know him as Mark's Son of God who transcends the heaven-earth divide, who belongs to the realm of the Father and the angels, and who has the supernatural power to destroy evil and unclean spirits. This might include Jesus as an idealized human figure who represents God's reign, but it also exceeds it.

39. Peppard, *Son of God*, 97. On the non-pre-existence of Jesus in Mark's Gospel, see e.g., Boring, *Mark*, 44.

14:62), exercises the prerogative of judgment (Mark 8:38), arbitrates the forgiveness of sins and redemption (Mark 2:10; 10:45), and establishes or renews the covenant (Mark 14:22–25).

The definitive reason against understanding the baptismal episode as an adoption is because the language of sonship is rehearsed later at the transfiguration (Mark 9:2–8) and again at the crucifixion (Mark 15:39). Mark envisages three christologically decisive moments in Jesus's career and no one of them is singularly determinative for Jesus's sonship. If a voice pronouncing Jesus as a "son" implies adoption, then Jesus is adopted an astounding three times in the course of Mark's Gospel: at his baptism, at the transfiguration, and at the crucifixion. Paul Vielhauer saw a gradual progression with Jesus's adoption (Mark 1:11), proclamation (Mark 9:7), and acclamation (Mark 15:39), but that was built on the assumption that Mark was following an Egyptian religious model, a spurious assumption at best.[40] What is more, if perchance Mark did have in mind a single moment when Jesus was adopted, the transfiguration and crucifixion scenes have a better claim to constituting the decisive moment of adoption. Compared to the baptism scene, the transfiguration is more dramatic and exhibits far more supernatural imagery to underscore Jesus's identity. As his clothes shine with heavenly radiance, Jesus is joined by the Israelite heroes of Elijah and Moses, and the divine voice not only affirms Jesus's sonship but urges the disciples to listen to him (Mark 9:2–8). Alternatively, during the crucifixion, Jesus expires in powerful fashion (Mark 15:37), there is a supernatural portent with the curtain of the temple torn in two (Mark 15:38), and in a piece of fierce irony Jesus is acclaimed as a Son of God by a Roman centurion (Mark 15:39). The crucifixion scene is a natural point for Jesus's adoption and deification since Roman emperors were always consecrated as *divus* after their deaths. In addition, the centurion's confession also marks out Jesus

---

40. Paul Vielhauer, "Erwägungen zur Christologie des Markusevangeliums," in *Zeit und Geschichte. Dankesgabe an Rudolf Bultmann zum 80. Geburtstag*, ed. Erich Dinkler (Tübingen: Mohr Siebeck, 1964), 166–68 ("Aber dieses Verständnis dürfte weder dem inneren Zusammenhang der drei Stellen noch der deutlich beabsichtigten Steigerung ganz gerecht werden; zu beachten ist, daß die drei Sätze ihrem formalen Charakter nach je eine bestimmte Funktion erfüllen [Adoption 1,11, Proklamation 9,7, Akklamation 15,39])" [166]).

as a counter-emperor to the Roman emperor who was also touted as a son of god. The heavenly voice at the baptism scene that declared Jesus "my beloved son," while certainly not insignificant, is eclipsed by the supernatural imagery and narrative climax that accompany the declarations of Jesus's divine sonship at the transfiguration and again at the crucifixion. In the end, I find it difficult to regard any of these as an adoption. Far more likely, we have three moments of divine revelation where, first, Jesus is commissioned in his role as the messianic son and servant of Israel (baptism). He is then revealed to be more glorious and superior to the status of exalted figures like Elijah and Moses (transfiguration).[41] Finally, Jesus is the royal-shepherd king who suffers injustice but dies a noble and self-giving death that even a centurion recognizes by acclaiming him as God's Son (crucifixion).

In sum, there is no adoption in the Gospel of Mark. The adoptionism suspected to lay behind Mark 1:9–11 has no more life setting in the early church than the alleged adoptionism wrongly presumed to lay behind Rom 1:3–4.[42]

Mark's Divine Christology

A further chink in the armor of the view that Mark has an adoptionist Christology is the evidence from the wider Markan narrative that, even amidst the human realism of Jesus's actions and emotions, ascribes transcendent qualities and a divine identity to Jesus. This transcendence means Jesus has a heavenly origin, while his divine identity is not acquired but

41. Contra Kirk, *A Man Attested by God*, 196–97, who thinks that Mark portrays Jesus here as an exalted figure the same as Moses and Elijah, making the story indicative of "Jesus's idealized humanity, not some sort of pre-existence or ontological divinity." To which I think Mark would respond, much like the writer to the Hebrews, by saying, "To which idealized human figure did God ever glorify in splendor and say, 'This is my Son, listen to him'?"

42. Here, I am echoing Peter Stuhlmacher, *Biblische Theologie des Neuen Testaments*, 2 vols. (Göttingen: Vandenhoeck & Ruprecht, 1992–1999), 1:187: "Die hinter Röm 1,3–4 vermutete adoptianische Zweistufenchristologie hat ebensowenig einen Sitz in Leben in Urchristentum wie der hinter Mark 1,9–11Par vermutete Adoptianismus."

JESUS THE ETERNAL SON

is intrinsic to his person. Jesus does not become divine as he is already divine.

It should be granted that the Markan Jesus is undoubtedly a divine agent who speaks and acts for God, even while his precise relationship to Israel's God is somewhat ambiguous. Howard Clark Kee asserts that Jesus's identification as the Son of Man and Messiah shows "the implied kinship of Jesus with God." Yet, what that kinship actually consists of is a mystery because, despite moments of revelation and public disclosures, Jesus's relationship to God is "implied rather than defined."[43] Daniel Kirk believes that Mark's Jesus has a "close proximity" to God, but there is also a "proximity in differentiation between Jesus and God" that is crucial for Mark's narrative.[44] Joel Marcus observes the dissonance in parts of the narrative like the prologue where there is "a strong impression of the relatedness of Jesus to God" and at the same time "a measure of acknowledgement of the distinction between them." He resolves this dissonance by way of an implied "subordination," which is true to the extent that Jesus is a divine agent of God's reign and redemption. However, such a description is inadequate when we remember that Jesus is portrayed as sharing in God's splendor and throne.[45] It is probably better to say, as Boring does, that Jesus and God the Father are more "parallel" than "subordinate."[46]

The nature of Jesus's relationship with God in the Gospel of Mark can be understood in terms of there being a weak, moderate, or strong degree of identification between the two.

For a weak correlation of Jesus and God, Stephen Ahearne-Kroll thinks the Markan presentation of Jesus "is at once powerful and Godlike, utterly human, and mediating between the divine and the human as a prophetic figure."[47] According to Kirk, Mark's Jesus is an idealized

---

43. Howard Clark Kee, "Christology in Mark's Gospel," in *Judaism and Their Messiahs at the Turn of the Christian Era*, ed. Jacob Neusner, William Scott Green, and Ernest S. Frerichs (Cambridge: Cambridge University Press, 1987), 201, 206.

44. Kirk, *Man Attested by God*, 499, 501.

45. Marcus, *Way of the Lord*, 39.

46. Boring, "Markan Christology," 458.

47. Stephen P. Ahearne-Kroll, "The Scripturally Complex Presentation of Jesus in the Gospel of Mark," in *Portraits of Jesus: Studies in Christology*, ed. Susan E. Meyers, WUNT 2.321 (Tübingen: Mohr Siebeck, 2012), 47–48.

human figure who embodies, mediates, and represents God and God's reign. In this sense, Jesus is identified *with* God but not *as* God. Thus, Kirk detects no "Christology of Jesus's ontological identity with YHWH" but more properly "a Christology of representation and even embodiment of the reality of YHWH's actions."[48] The distinguishing trait here is divine agency rather than divine identity.

On the moderate side, Hays contends that "Mark's Gospel suggests that Jesus is, in some way that defies comprehension, the embodiment of God's presence." Further to that, "His central character, Jesus, seems to be at the same time—if we may put it crudely—both the God of Israel and a human being not simply identical with the God of Israel. Thus, Mark's story already poses the riddles that the church's theologians later sought to solve in the Christological controversies of the fourth and fifth centuries. The logical tensions are internal to Mark's account; they are not created only when we set the 'divine' Jesus of the Fourth Gospel in contrast to the 'human' Jesus of the Synoptics."[49] Hays sees in Mark a genuinely strong identification of Jesus with God, but he is sufficiently aware of the ambiguities that the Markan presentation of Jesus carries, which suggest divine identity with a strong sense of ambiguity. Michael Whitenton detects in Mark both vestiges of adoptionism but also an "assimilation" between Mark's Jesus and the behaviors and qualities of God so that Jesus is "cast as a god-in-disguise, a divine being, who is functionally equivalent to Yahweh in the Markan narrative."[50]

In contrast, others argue for a stronger identification between Jesus and God, more than embodiment or agency, but concrete identification. Mark's depiction of the Son of Man is such that, for Philip Davis, "[A] major element in Mark's understanding of the passion is expressed in terms of the dichotomy between Jesus, the man who is on God's side, and 'men.' Again, Jesus appears as a surrogate for God."[51] Elsewhere the disclosure of Jesus's divine sonship in tandem with Jesus's role as the

48. Kirk, *A Man Attested by God*, 501.

49. Hays, *Reading Backwards*, 19, 27–28. See similarly Boring, *Mark*, 44: "*How* it is that Jesus is both from God and from Nazareth Mark leaves as an unnarrated, unconceptualized mystery" (italics original).

50. Whitenton, *Hearing Kyriotic Sonship*, 3–4.

51. Davis, "Mark's Christological Paradox," 171–72.

future judge lends itself to the suggestion of the Markan Jesus's "intrinsic divinity."[52]

I am convinced, following Robert Gundry, that the Gospel of Mark is largely an apology for a crucified Messiah.[53] Thus, Mark's purpose is to show that Jesus is the Messiah not despite the cross but, rather, precisely because of it. However, along the way Mark constructs his portrait of Jesus in such a way that strongly suggests that Jesus is part of the divine identity: he speaks and acts for God in such a way that the lines between divine sender and human agent are blurred and ambiguous. Mark's Gospel constitutes a mutation of Jewish monotheism whereby a human agent is independent of God and yet concomitantly reckoned to be co-equal to the divine subject.

Markan κύριος Language for Jesus

A first feature we should investigate is the κύριος language used for Jesus across the Gospel of Mark. In some cases this language clearly refers to Israel's God as distinct from Jesus (Mark 11:9; 12:9, 11, 29–30), elsewhere it is ambiguous as to whether God or Jesus is the intended referent (e.g., Mark 5:19; 11:3; 13:20), and in other instances Jesus is described in such a way that he and the God of Israel both share in the identity of the κύριος (Mark 1:3; 2:28; 12:35–37; 13:35).[54]

Mark's description of Jesus as the "Messiah" in the incipit (Mark 1:1) is not limited to Jesus's role as a Davidic deliverer, but also extends to his being akin to the "Lord" and the "angel of the Lord," as the subsequent prologue with its scriptural citations makes clear (Mark 1:2–3). Mark invites readers familiar with the Septuagint to draw the inference that the introduction of Jesus into the story is the arrival of the Lord who comes to save his people in a new exodus.[55]

52. Davis, "Mark's Christological Paradox," 175.
53. Robert H. Gundry, *Mark: A Commentary on His Apology for the Cross* (Grand Rapids: Eerdmans, 1993), followed by Bird, *Jesus is the Christ*, 55–56, and Craig A. Evans, *Mark 8:27–16:20*, WBC (Nashville, TX: Nelson, 2001), xciii.
54. Daniel Johansson, "*Kyrios* in the Gospel of Mark," *JSNT* 33 (2010): 101–24.
55. Whitenton, *Hearing Kyriotic Sonship*, 108.

Just as it is written in Isaiah the prophet, "Behold, I am sending my messenger before your face (προσώπου σου), who will prepare your way; the voice of one crying out in the wilderness: 'Prepare the way of the Lord (κύριος), make his paths straight'" (Mark 1:2–3).

Behold, *I am sending my messenger* and he will prepare *the way* before my face, and *the Lord* whom you seek will suddenly come to his temple. The *angel of the covenant* in whom you delight—indeed, behold *he is coming,* says the Lord of hosts. (Mal 3:1)	Behold, *I am sending my angel before your face*, to guard you *on the way* and to bring you to the place that I have prepared. Be careful to heed him and listen to his voice; do not rebel against him, for he will not pardon your transgression, for my name is in him. (Exod 23:20–21)	A voice cries out: "In the wilderness prepare the way of the Lord, make straight in the desert a highway for our God." (Isa 40:3)

The Markan prologue with its composite citation of Mal 3:1, Exod 23:20–21, and Isa 40:3[56] amounts to a "transcendent offstage voice" declaring that the story about to be heard accords with Scripture, specifically, Isaiah.[57] We can note a few things from this: (1) The Malachi text is looking to a period in Israel's post-exilic restoration that is prepared by the "angel of the covenant" and climaxes in the Lord himself coming to the temple.[58] (2) Malachi is arguably alluding to Exod 23:20–21 where the Lord sent his angel to lead the Hebrews in their sojourn through the wilderness, and the angel embodies the presence of God's name, Yahweh. (3) The Markan citation ends with the Isaianic promise that God will come and lead the

---

56. On composite citations, see Sean A. Adams and Seth M. Ehorn, "What is a Composite Citation? An Introduction," in *Composite Citations in Antiquity*, vol. 1: *Jewish, Graeco-Roman, and Early Christian Uses*, ed. Sean A. Adams and Seth M. Ehorn, LNTS 525 (London: Bloomsbury, 2016), 1–16.

57. Boring, *Mark*, 34–35.

58. How the angel of the covenant, the Lord, and the eschatological Elijah relate to each other in Malachi 3–4 is an open question.

exilic remnant in a new exodus that is first heralded by a prophetic voice in the wilderness.

In the context of Mark 1:2–8, the "messenger" and "voice" is obviously John the Baptist, and while the "Lord" would naturally lead one to think it is the God of Israel, the introduction of Jesus immediately after clarifies that this Lord is none other than Jesus. He is the "Lord" whose arrival the messenger is to prepare for. John prepares the way for the coming "Lord," and the Lord who comes is Jesus.[59] The application of the composite quotation is that Jesus is not only the Messiah, but Malachi's "Lord" and "angel of the covenant," functionally equivalent to the "angel" of the divine presence who accompanied Israel in the exodus, and in terms of Isaiah, the presence of Yahweh himself.[60] Before readers learn anything about Jesus's career and life, they are informed in the prologue that Jesus is the transcendent Lord who has a "way" in this world.[61] Paul Owen sums up the significance of the composite citation:

> For Mark, the "Lord/God," whose way is prepared by the "voice" in the wilderness (John the Baptist) according to Isaiah, is more specifically the "angel of the covenant" (Mal 3:1) in whom the name YHWH resides (Exod 23:21), whose arrival is preceded by "Elijah" in Malachi's eschatology. The angel of YHWH will lead God's people out of the spiritual exile safely to Zion in a second exodus (cf. Isa 40:9–11).[62]

If John the Baptist prepares the way for one who is already named as "Lord" in Mark 1:3, then the heavenly voice can only be *identifying* Jesus as God's Son at his baptism, not *elevating* him to divine sonship in Mark 1:11.[63]

Later, in one of the conflict stories concerning Jesus and the Sabbath, Jesus responds to his Pharisaic opponents that flouting their halakhah is

---

59. Cf. Rudolf Pesch, *Das Markusevangelium*, 2 vols, HThKNT (Freiburg im Breisgau: Herder, 1976–1977), 1:77; Collins, *Mark*, 137; France, *Mark*, 64; Boring, *Mark*, 36–37.

60. Rikki Watts, *Isaiah's New Exodus and Mark*, WUNT 99 (Tübingen: Mohr/Siebeck, 1997), 87.

61. Boring, *Mark*, 36.

62. Owen, "Jesus as God's Chief Agent," 43.

63. Owen, "Jesus as God's Chief Agent," 56.

justified because the Son of Man is Lord even of the Sabbath (Mark 2:28). This logion could be saying no more than the Sabbath's purpose in helping humanity (v. 27) implies humanity's authority over the Sabbath (playing on the sense of "Son of Man" as a Semitic idiom for "human being"). Alternatively, in light of the conflict described in Mark 2:23–28, it might imply that the Son of Man holds a special authority over the Sabbath and therefore can define its purpose and proper application. In favor of the latter view, we can say a few things: (1) It would be exceedingly odd for Jesus or Mark to think that human beings in general, even if restricted to Israel, possesses authority to decide for themselves under what circumstances they may override the Sabbath command. Rights to abrogate the Sabbath are particularly affronting when one remembers that the Scriptures attribute such an authority to Yahweh as the one who instituted and consecrated the day of rest (see Exod 16:22–30; 20:10–11; 31:15–17; Lev 23:1–11; Deut 5:12–15), which is why Yahweh calls it "my Sabbath" (Exod 31:13; Lev 19:3, 30; Ezek 20:12–13). (2) If we compare Mark 2:23–28 with 2:1–10, then we see an emerging pattern in these conflict stories where Jesus's provocative action ends with an emphatic statement about Jesus's own particular authority (2:10 and 2:28) that justifies his controversial behavior. (3) The parallel texts in Matthew and Luke are even more unequivocal that Jesus's authority over the Sabbath is not a general human authority. Rather, it is uniquely his authority as the Son of Man that is stressed (Matt 12:6; Luke 6:5). We might paraphrase the Markan Jesus's reasoning: "You forget that the Sabbath was instituted to meet a human need so human needs may override sabbatarian restrictions. I declare this as no meagre opinion nor as a mere beneficiary of the Sabbath's command to rest, but as one who is the Lord of the Sabbath, so I may legitimately pronounce when it is appropriate to suspend its requirements." If this is the case, as Gundry observes: "A Christological point has grown out of an anthropological one, and outgrown it."[64] If Jesus carries authority over the most sacred and holy of divinely created institutions, then, as France puts it: "The christological stakes could hardly be pitched higher than this."[65]

Another example of κύριος language is the story of Jesus's encoun-

---

64. Gundry, *Mark*, 145.
65. France, *Mark*, 148.

ter with the Gerasene demoniac. At the end of the story we read in Mark 5:19–20: "[Jesus] said to him, 'Go home to your people, and tell them how much the Lord has done for you, and what mercy he has displayed toward you [ὅσα ὁ κύριός σοι πεποίηκεν καὶ ἠλέησέν σε].' And he went away and began to proclaim in the Decapolis how much Jesus had done for him [ὅσα ἐποίησεν αὐτῷ ὁ Ἰησοῦς]." Jesus instructs the demoniac to tell his family and friends what the "Lord" had done for him, but his reflexive action is to announce what Jesus has done for him. On the one hand, this could mean nothing more than Jesus is the agent of the Lord and acts in his name and with his power. However, it is interesting that the only other usage of ἐλεέω ("I have mercy") is when Jesus is the object of a petition for mercy (Mark 10:47–48). It would be incorrect to infer that Mark conflates Jesus and God; even so, it is reasonable to surmise that Jesus and God modulate together under the designation κύριός.[66] In the very least, the Markan Jesus's exorcistic activity must be understood in light of his identity as "Lord."[67] Ultimately, it is through Jesus that the merciful work of the Lord is experienced and encountered.

The pericopae in Mark 12:28–35 encapsulate many of the paradoxes in Markan Christology where we find a clear and concise affirmation of monotheism in conjunction with a christological redefinition of monotheism that places the Messiah within the identity of Israel's κύριος. When asked what is the most important command, Jesus responds by affirming the Shema from Deut 6:4–5 with "The Lord our God, the Lord is one" (κύριος ὁ θεὸς ἡμῶν κύριος εἷς ἐστιν) that leads into the second greatest command about love of neighbor with a citation of Lev 19:18 (Mark 12:29–31). Whatever Mark thinks of Jesus vis-à-vis God, clearly Jesus is not a second god, a lesser god, or even a demi-god, because Mark knows there is only one God and one Lord of Israel (see also Mark 2:7; 10:18). Boring comments: "It is important to Mark, however, to emphasize that the Christian community's Christological use of God-language for Jesus is not an infringement on monotheism, important not only in its dialogue with Judaism, but with the polytheistic pagan world."[68] And yet Mark,

---

66. Boring, *Mark*, 154, followed by Johansson, *"Kyrios* in the Gospel of Mark," 106.
67. Whitenton, *Hearing Kyriotic Sonship*, 186.
68. Boring, *Mark*, 346.

much like Paul in 1 Cor 8:6, takes the Shema about the "Lord is one" and redefines it by immediately narrating an exchange between Jesus and the scribes. As a result, Jesus is identified as one of two κύριοι in Ps 110:1 (Mark 12:35–37). Jesus is not less than a Son of David, but certainly a whole lot more as the messianic κύριος.

The messianic riddle pertains to Jesus's question to the scribes as to how the Messiah can be a Son of David when David speaking in Ps 110:1 calls the Messiah "Lord." The unit has prompted several questions as to whether Jesus is denying that the Messiah is a Son of David or whether he, though not a Son of David, is still the Messiah. Yet much of this discussion simply misses the primary point of the unit.[69] The operating assumption is that David is the speaker of the psalm and he describes how "the Lord" (i.e., Yahweh) addresses the Messiah, whom David calls "my Lord," so that the eschatological Son of David must be more than a future descendent from the Davidic line. Jesus is asserting that while the Messiah is a Son of David, he is more than a biological descendent of David; the Messiah has pre-existence since Yahweh addresses him in David's time, he has divine sovereignty as κύριος and priestly authority on par with Melchizedek, as Ps 110:1–4 makes clear. That the Messiah is superior to David is clear enough,[70] but how the messianic κύριος precisely relates to Yahweh is less so. We have already seen that Israel has only one κύριος (Mark 12:28–32), and yet Jesus is another κύριος who shares Yahweh's throne (Mark 12:35–37; cf. 14:62). It is perhaps tempting to see Jesus as a subordinated κύριος, lesser than Yahweh yet greater than David. However, standard monotheistic formulas are explicit in their affirmation that "there is no other Lord/God except him," which does not countenance the possibility of a miniature throne buddy who comes under the moniker κύριος (Deut 4:35, 39; Isa 44:8; 45:5–6, 18–22; 46:9). On top of that, the position at a deity's "right hand" in ancient iconography and texts implied co-regency not inferiority (see Dan 7:9–14; b. Sanhedrin 38b).[71] According to Joel Marcus, the net

69. See Bird, *Are You the One Who Is to Come?* 130–32; Bird, *Jesus is the Christ*, 53–54.

70. Kee, "Christology in Mark's Gospel," 203, comments: "The messianic figure does not merely model the Davidic paradigm but surpasses David in a transcendent manner."

71. On Roman emperors at the right hand of a deity, see Evans, *Mark*, lxxvii. For imagery in the Ancient Near East, see Whitenton, *Hearing Kyriotic Sonship*, 231 n. 97.

effect of sharing Yahweh's throne is that Jesus "stands in a relation of near-equality with God, and the inference for Mark would seem to be that Jesus is not (just) the Son of David but (also) the Son of God. This implication is consonant with the continuation of Ps 110 in the LXX that speaks of divine begetting (Ps 110:3 [109:3 LXX])."[72] I think the solution to the tension is that Deut 6:4 (Mark 12:29) certainly restricts the meaning of κύριος to a stringent monotheism, yet the placement of Jesus within Ps 110:1 (Mark 12:36–37) serves to redefine that monotheism in light of Jesus's person and work. Mark's monotheism will not countenance ditheism or subordinationism. Yet, Jesus is placed in the orbit of Israel's κύριος. Viewed this way, it is better to regard Mark's double identification of God and Jesus as κύριος within the accumulated ambiguity about the identity of Israel's κύριος that has developed since Mark 1:2–3. Mark's narrative defines the way of the κύριος as the way of Jesus Christ, so that there is one κύριος who is split between two distinct persons of God and Jesus, both share this name and title.[73]

The Olivet Discourse presents Jesus as both a prophet delivering an oracle of judgment but also as the divine figure, the "Lord" and "Son of Man," who will enact a catastrophic judgment with the destruction of the Jerusalem temple. To begin with, the various travails associated with the tribulation are said to be of a degree never seen since God (θεός) "created the world" and "never to be equaled again" (Mark 13:19). Respite is possible only because the "Lord" (κύριος) will cut short the days to enable the elect to survive (Mark 13:20). My contention is that the "God" of verse 19 is differentiated from the "Lord" of verse 20 by virtue of their respective functions of creation and judgment. Such a prospect is enhanced when we observe that Jesus is the central figure in the discourse who stands against those who impersonate him (Mark 13:5–6, 21–22), who oppose him and his people (Mark 13:9–13), and who in turn rescues the elect (Mark 13:13, 20, 27). In addition, toward the very end of the Olivet Discourse, Mark narrates the parabolic exhortation, "Therefore keep watch because you do not know when the Lord of the house (ὁ κύριος τῆς οἰκίας) will return—

---

72. Joel Marcus, *Mark 8–16: A New Translation with Introduction and Commentary*, AYB (New Haven: Yale University Press, 2007), 850–51.

73. Johansson, "*Kyrios* in the Gospel of Mark," 119.

whether in the evening, or at midnight, or when the rooster crows, or at dawn" (Mark 13:35). The κύριος is most likely the Son of Man, who comes to bring judgment on Jerusalem and to gather the elect. Similar language was used earlier concerning a time when the Son of Man "comes in his Father's glory with the holy angels" to judge those ashamed of him (Mark 8:38). It is also used immediately preceding in the description of the days of suffering ending with "the Son of Man coming in clouds with great power and glory" to rescue his elect (Mark 13:26). And of course, similar language appears later during the trial where Jesus warns that he will judge the Sanhedrin in a heavenly courtroom as the "Son of Man sitting at the right hand of the Mighty One and coming on the clouds of heaven" (Mark 14:62). If we take the κύριος references of Mark 13:20 and 35 together with the theophanic language of Mark 8:38, 13:26, and 14:62 about the Son of Man, then the pictures that emerges is that Jesus is the κύριός of the future judgment. The implication is that Jesus is the coming κύριός who exercises judgment and is enthroned beside God. The intertextual echoes and narrative rhetoric within the Olivet Discourse is such that the Markan Jesus "is the Danielic Son of Man transfigured by the eschatological hope of the Jewish Scriptures—the return of YHWH to his people."[74]

We may conclude from this that Jesus is intrinsic to the identity of Israel's κύριος, who has come to effect a new exodus for Israel and to bring deliverance to the nations by ushering in the kingdom of God. God does not retreat from the narrative when Jesus appears, but remains active and distinct from Jesus, and yet God and Jesus both go under the mantle κύριος and sovereign roles are shared between them. Mark exhibits a sophisticated yet paradoxical κύριος Christology. Based on this Marcus concludes: "The Markan view of the relation between Jesus and the κύριος, then, subtly combines a recognition of the separateness of the two figures with a recognition of their inseparability. Perhaps the best way to express this complex relationship is to say that, in Mark, where Jesus acts, there the Lord is powerfully at work."[75] Johansson is similar, but he rightly sees a more concrete identification between Jesus and the κύριος: "The exclu-

---

74. Joshua E. Leim, "In the Glory of the Father: Intertextuality and the Apocalyptic Son of Man in the Gospel of Mark," *JTI* 7 (2013): 219.

75. Marcus, *Way of the Lord*, 39–40.

sive divinity of the God of Israel is maintained, but not to the exclusion of Jesus. If we ask who the κύριος in the Gospel of Mark is, the paradoxical answer is: God and Jesus."[76]

Jesus's Divine Prerogative in Forgiving Sins

A second feature we should note is that the Markan Jesus exercises a divine prerogative in forgiving people of their sins.

In the story of Jesus's healing a paralytic and forgiving him of his sins, Jesus's action leads to a charge of blasphemy by the on-looking scribes to the effect that Jesus has done what only God can do (Mark 2:1–12, esp. 2:7). Several scholars suggest that forgiving sins was hardly inappropriate for a human when undertaking certain religious offices like a priest since priests would ordinarily pronounce the forgiveness of sins after ritual sacrifices. Ehrman accordingly takes this story to mean that "Jesus may be claiming a priestly prerogative, but not a divine one."[77] There are, unfortunately, two problems here.[78]

First, no evidence exists that the priest ever pronounced the forgiveness of sins before, during, or after the offering of sacrifices.[79] The ancient texts that describe Jewish sacrificial ceremonies in the temple do not mention priestly pronouncement of absolution for sins (see Lev 1–7; 16–17; 22–23; Let. Arist. 95; Sir 50.5–21; m. Yoma). There is no evidence that priests ritually declared the absolution of sins over a sacrifice or that they themselves forgave sins in God's stead.[80] The priests performed cultic rites to make atonement for their sins and for those of the people, but the

76. Johansson, "*Kyrios* in the Gospel of Mark," 121.

77. Ehrman, *How Jesus Became God*, 127.

78. What follows is heavily indebted to the superb article by Daniel Johannsson, "'Who Can Forgive Sins but God Alone?' Human and Angelic Agents, and Divine Forgiveness in Early Judaism" *JSNT* 33 (2011): 351–74.

79. So too Tobias Hägerland, *Jesus and the Forgiveness of Sins: An Aspect of His Prophetic Mission*, SNTSMS 150 (Cambridge: Cambridge University Press, 2012), 132–42.

80. On the role of the high priest in ritually removing the sins of Israelites through the cultus, see Exod 28:38 and Lev 10:17. Yet we should observe that issues of authority are not raised and no pronouncement is ever said to have been made.

authority to forgive sins remained with God himself.[81] One must wonder if the interpreters who claim that Jesus was simply acting in a priestly fashion—a view which, I must confess, I formerly assumed myself—have haphazardly read Mark 2:7 in light of later Christian liturgy, where priests declare absolution for sins after the public confession of sin during a worship service, and then projected this Christian conception of the priestly office back into Israelite priesthood.

Second, Mark's narration of the story does not remotely raise the prospect of an incursion into the priestly office by a non-priest. The affront of the scribes was not that Jesus was acting like a rogue priest. They do not complain, "Who can forgive sins but a priest alone?" Jesus is not alleged to have transgressed the priestly vocation, but to have made a divine pronouncement in a manner that was perceived to usurp a divine prerogative, which equated to blasphemy by some definitions.[82] Jesus has transgressed something that pertains exclusively and uniquely to the "one God" (Mark 2:7): forgiving or remitting sins.[83] In fact, there is an interesting parallel to the scribes' statement in Mark 2:7 in a Midrash on Ps. 17 where the author has David say to God, "No one can forgive sins but you alone" (m. Ps. 17.3).

---

81. On God forgiving sins, see e.g., Exod 34:6–7; Deut 29:20; Ps 25:18; Isa 43:25–26; Jer 31:34; Dan 9:9; Mic 7:18–20.

82. See Evans, *Mark*, 453–58.

83. Crispin H. T. Fletcher-Louis, "Jesus as the High Priestly Messiah: Part 2," *JSHJ* 5 (2007): 71–74, thinks that Daniel's Son of Man was an eschatological high priest and Jesus's authority to forgive is really an extension of the authority given to the Son of Man in Dan 7:14. He also gives the example in 2 Enoch where Enoch is appointed as a priest (2 En. 22.8–10) and later revered as one whom God "appointed . . . to be the one who carried away the sin of mankind" (2 En. 64.5). The priestly connotation of Daniel's "one like a Son of Man" are generally interesting, though perhaps somewhat speculative. However, I would protest that: (1) there is no indication in Mark 2:1–10 that Jesus has been *appointed* to forgive, nor is there a sense of delegation or mediation—the shocking thing in the pericope is that Jesus speaks with unmediated authority; (2) Jesus does not appear to be offering the forgiveness or remission of sins connected with any temple or cultus, be it the real temple or an eschatological temple, which sets him apart from the domain of normal priestly functions; and (3) we need to add that simply because a figure, whether Aaron or Enoch, is appointed to facilitate the forgiveness/remission/bearing-away of sins (the terms are ambiguous in themselves), it does not necessarily entail any particular authority or power inherent on their part—rather, the ritual is *ex opere operato* because it is divinely instituted.

In which case, a man who claims to do what only God can do attempts to undermine God's unique authority and that is what leads to the charge of blasphemy. As France says, "To claim to do what only God could do, and to constitute himself God's spokesman in declaring sins forgiven, was to infringe the divine prerogative."[84]

It is significant that Mark's Jesus, unperturbed by the reasoning of the scribe, proceeds with the healing "in order that you may know that the Son of Man has authority on earth to forgive sins" (Mark 2:10). Jesus does not assuage their concern by distinguishing his agency from God's authority; rather, he equates the Son of Man's authority to forgive with the authority of this "one God." Thereafter Jesus commands the paralytic man to stand up, pick up his mat, and to go home. Even more astounding, the man can and does precisely as Jesus instructs him. A miraculous healing takes place. Jesus claims for himself an unmediated divine authority that, to those steeped in Jewish monotheism, looked absolutely blasphemous. And yet, nonetheless, the paralytic man is healed. The bite of Jesus's rhetoric is that he is proven right. *If* he can make a paralytic walk, *then* he has the divine authority of the "one God" to pronounce the forgiveness of sins.[85]

Jesus and Theophanic Episodes

A third feature of the Markan narrative requiring consideration is the theophanic episodes where Jesus exercises God's power over creation

---

84. France, *Mark*, 126. Similar is Marcus, *Way of the Lord*, 40: "The forgiveness of sins which Jesus exercises in his capacity as Son of Man reflects God's own prerogative."

85. Kirk, *A Man Attested by God*, 272–81, errs in his treatment of this passage by again contending that it merely represents Jesus as an idealized human figure. Against Kirk (274), when John the Baptist declared a baptism for the forgiveness of sins the implied forgiver was God, whereas in this story the Son of Man is the forgiver based on an unmediated divine authority to forgive. Jesus does not proclaim the necessary work for God to forgive sins; rather, he forgives sins on his own authority, without ritual or repentance, by pure fiat. For Kirk's thesis to work he has to assume that the scribes were wrong in their accusation of blasphemy because God alone does not have the authority to forgive sins (279). But the rhetorical bite of the Markan narrative is that the scribes are right, only God can forgive sins, but they do not connect the dots as Mark expects his readers to.

and appears in divine glory. Naturally, we can look to the sea miracles where Jesus calms the storm (Mark 4:35–41) and walks on the water (Mark 6:45–52) in a manner that harks back to scriptural images for Yahweh's authority over the sea.

When Jesus and the disciples are caught in the midst of a furious squall in their small boat on the Sea of Galilee, they are fearful and one of them rouses Jesus from his slumber in the stern of the vessel. Mark reports: "He got up, rebuked the wind and said to the waves, 'Silence! Be still!' Then the wind died down and it was completely calm" (Mark 4:39). Jesus's command over the sea alludes to Ps 107, a text that describes Yahweh as the redeemer of the people, who preserves those in all sorts of predicaments, including seafarers:

> Some went out on the sea in ships; they were merchants on the mighty waters.
> They saw the works of the LORD, his wonderful deeds in the deep.
> For he spoke and stirred up a tempest that lifted high the waves.
> They mounted up to the heavens and went down to the depths; in their peril their courage melted away.
> They reeled and staggered like drunkards; they were at their wits' end.
> Then they cried out to the LORD in their trouble, and he brought them out of their distress.
> He stilled the storm to a whisper; the waves of the sea were hushed.
> They were glad when it grew calm, and he guided them to their desired haven.
> (Ps 107:23–30 [NIV])[86]

In response to the calming of the storm, the disciples shift from terror at the storm to terror at Jesus's power over the elements, and they ask, "Who is this, that even the wind and the waves obey him?" If a scripturally attuned reader familiar with texts like Ps 107 or even Jonah had to volunteer an answer to this question, he or she might answer that "Jesus has shown godlike superiority over the elements."[87] Or, as Adela Collins comments,

---

86. See also Ps 65:5–7 and Job 9:8–11.
87. Hurtado, *Lord Jesus Christ*, 285–86.

"The narrative thus portrays Jesus behaving not like a devout human person but like God, who caused the sea to cease from its raging in the Jonah story. Thus, Jesus is portrayed not so much as a human being who has trust in God's power to save, but as a divine being."[88] A similar observation is made by Whitenton, "As the sailors cry out to their own gods in Jonah 1:5 LXX and the sailors of Ps 107:4 LXX to Yahweh, so the disciples turn to the Markan Jesus (Mark 4:38). . . . Thus, while the Markan Jesus begins the scene as Jonah, the episode closes with him as Jonah's God."[89] Beyond that, there might be further counter-imperial significance. Philo summarizes general acclaim for Augustus as pacifying the elements under his reign, "And this is Caesar, who calmed the storms that were raging in every direction, who healed the common diseases that were afflicting Greeks and Barbarians."[90] It is sufficient to say that Jesus appears to exhibit Yahweh-like control over the sea and rivals any of the rhetoric for Caesar's control over the elements. Hays thinks that the disciples' fearful question, "Who is this that even the wind and the sea obey him?" (Mark 4:41) requires a divine answer: "For any reader versed in Israel's Scripture: there can be only one possible answer: it is the Lord God of Israel who has the power to command wind and sea and to subdue the chaotic forces of nature."[91]

The Markan version of Jesus walking on the water (Mark 6:45–52) is similarly saturated with scriptural allusions for Yahweh's person and power. The miraculous feat of walking on the water itself recalls Job's description of God as one who "alone stretches out the heavens and treads on the waves of the sea" (Job 9:8). More prominently we encounter several Yahweh traditions, specifically, those associated with the exodus, echoed in the story. When Jesus was walking on the lake, Mark tells us that Jesus intended to "pass them by" (Mark 6:48), which is reminiscent of Yahweh passing through the waters ahead of Israel in the exodus (Ps 77:19; Isa 43:2) and Yahweh passing by Moses, who was hid in the cleft of the rock,

---

88. Collins, *Mark*, 260. See similarly Marcus, *Way of the Lord*, 144–45: "He [Jesus] is speaking in and acting out the language of the Old Testament divine warrior theophanies, narratives in which Yahweh himself subdues the demonic forces of chaos in a saving, cosmos-creating act of holy war."

89. Whitenton, *Hearing Kyriotic Sonship*, 178.

90. Philo, *Legat.* 145 (translation mine).

91. Hays, *Reading Backwards*, 22.

to reveal the divine glory to him (Exod 33:18–23). Although Jesus had intended to pass by the disciples (Mark 6:48), he had to divert on account of the disciples' fear that they were witnessing a ghost (Mark 6:49). Jesus responds by climbing into the boat, at which time the wild weather ceases, and he encourages them with the words, "Be of good cheer, I am, do not be afraid." The Johanninesque pronouncement "I am" (ἐγώ εἰμι) could be a pedestrian expression for "It is me" (see John 9:9), but in the context of the whole theophanic quality of the story it is hard to miss the allusions to the divine name (see Exod 3:13–15; Isa 41:10; 43:10–13, 25; 45:6, 18, 22; 48:12). Such an allusion is all the more plausible when we remember that in Deutero-Isaiah mentions of the divine name are often accompanied with exhortations not to be afraid (Isa 41:10, 13; 43:1, 5, etc.). In which case, the walking on water, the passing by, saying ἐγώ εἰμι, and telling the disciples not to be afraid—everything here—invokes Jesus as the personified presence and power of Yahweh from biblical tradition. Marcus rightly surmises that "the overwhelming impact by our narrative is an impression of divinity."[92]

We should also mention the transfiguration scene since it also has a certain theophanic quality in its description of Jesus. The transfiguration (Mark 9:2–8) is not a preview of Jesus's resurrection or parousia,[93] not the manifestation of Jesus as a Hellenistic deity. Rather, it is a divine disclosure of Jesus's heavenly identity built largely around the biblical theophany tradition (see Exod 34). His face does not shine as in Matt 17:2 and Luke 9:29. According to Mark, only his clothing radiates in a manner reminiscent of how departed saints are described as wearing brightly shining white garments (see Dan 12:3; Rev 4:4; 7:9; 1 *En.* 62.15). The transformation of Jesus's clothes into something whiter than any launderer on earth could wash them reflects a heavenly rather than earthly whiteness.[94] Bauckham surveys the motif of dazzlingly bleached clothing in Jewish literature and notes: "The basic idea behind all these descriptions is that heaven and its inhabitants are shining and bright. Hence the descriptions employ a stock series of images of brightness: heavenly beings or their

92. Marcus, *Mark 1–8*, 432.

93. Contra e.g., Pesch, *Das Markusevangelium*, 2:72–74.

94. Pesch, *Das Markusevangelium*, 2:73: "Jesus' splendor is not merely an earthly splendor" ("Jesus Glanz ist nicht mehr irdischer Glanz").

dress are typically shinning like the sun or the stars, gleaming like bronze or precious stones, fiery bright like torches or lightning, dazzling white like snow or pure wool."[95] The imagery amounts to a visual verification of Jesus's claim in Mark 8:38 that he is the Son of Man who will come in the glory of his Father with the holy angels.[96] Moreover, Jesus speaks to Moses and Elijah, not as if it is an introduction, but converses with him like he already knows them, like he knows where they are from, and like he knows them from where they are from: the heavenly realm. Jesus belongs in the company of famous scriptural heroes who were said to have been exalted to heaven.[97] Interesting too is that the divine voice from heaven that commands the disciples to "Listen to him" might allude to the scriptural exhortation for the Hebrews to heed and obey the "angel of the presence" in Exod 23:20–21, alluded to earlier in the prologue. As Jesus leads the disciples in the new exodus, he should be obeyed like the angel of the Lord in the old exodus.[98]

The Markan Jesus's Divine Authority

Coming to the fourth point, the Markan Jesus has a unique and unmediated sense of divine authority. We have already seen that Jesus possesses divine authority to forgive sins (Mark 2:10), authority over the Sabbath (Mark 2:28), and authority over the wind and sea (Mark 4:39), all of which indicate something more than prophetic authority. He possesses a power that extends over Israel's covenantal stipulations and even over all of creation. Beyond that, in the Olivet Discourse, Jesus makes two particular claims about the destruction of Jerusalem.

95. Richard Bauckham, "The Throne of God and the Worship of Jesus," in *The Jewish Roots of Christological Monotheism*, ed. Carey C. Newman, James R. Davila, and Gladys S. Lewis (Leiden: Brill, 1999), 51.

96. Evans, *Mark*, 36.

97. Collins, *Mark*, 423. On Moses's translation to heaven see Philo, *QG* 1.86; Josephus, *A.J.* 4.326; on Elijah's translation to heaven see 2 Kgdms 2:9–12; Josephus, *A.J.* 9.28; Sir 48.9.

98. There might also be echoes of the prophet-like-Moses in Deut 18:15 whom the Israelites are also commanded to listen to.

First, his words about the end will endure beyond the dissolution of the heavenly and terrestrial domains: "Heaven and earth will pass away, but my words will never pass away" (Mark 13:31). This is reminiscent of Isaianic language for the enduring power of divine revelation ("The grass withers and the flowers fall, but the word of our God endures forever" [Isa 40:8]). Jesus's λόγοι are thus put on a par with God's word in terms of its authority and permanence.[99] This is largely indicative of a wider theme in the Markan tradition, namely, that Jesus speaks and acts with an unprecedented sense of immediate divine authority (see Mark 1:22, 27; 2:10; 3:15; 4:41; 6:7; 11:27–33).

Second, on the timing of the end, Jesus professes ignorance: "But concerning that day or hour no one knows, not even the angels in heaven, nor the Son, but only the Father" (Mark 13:32). The saying is remarkable for its insistence on the limitation of Jesus's humanity in not knowing the divine moment assigned for the end. The saying caused mind-melting problems for later theologians of the church, and even scribes succumbed to the temptation to excise the phrase "nor the Son" from the Matthean parallel, and Luke omits the verse entirely. What is interesting for our purposes is that the saying places Jesus as part of a heavenly council with God and the angels. It is possible that this could be read as listing a heavenly hierarchy of Father – Son – Angels, but it is not demanded by the text. Whereas one might expect heavenly beings like angels and the Son to be privy to the secrets of the divine council, they are hereto unawares of the exact timing for the end in the Father's purpose. Despite their access to the divine council, God has kept it secret even from them. The embarrassment of Jesus's ignorance aside, the presupposition of the logion is that Jesus is a heavenly being like God and the angels.[100]

If we take Mark 13:31 and 32 together, we have a strong statement about Jesus as the bearer of divine authority and his place in heavenly authority among God and the angels.

Finally, we see something of Jesus's authority in the trial narrative where Jesus is described in such a way that he is destined to share God's throne in his post-resurrection state (Mark 14:61–64).[101] The whole trial

99. France, *Mark*, 540.
100. Gathercole, *The Preexistent Son*, 50, 272–73.
101. What follows is drawn from Michael F. Bird, "Did Jesus Think He Was God?" in *How God Became Jesus*, ed. Michael F. Bird (Grand Rapids: Zondervan, 2014), 65–66.

scene in the Gospels is a morass of textual, historical, and theological issues.[102] Suffice to say, it is quite plausible that at his trial Jesus was asked directly by the high priest if the rumors were true. Was he claiming to be the Messiah? Jesus answers obliquely, but affirmatively, and proceeds to describe himself as one who will be enthroned with Yahweh. The charge of blasphemy that Jesus's words elicit does not come from Jesus pronouncing the divine name, the Tetragrammaton "Yahweh," when he says, "I am." More probably it comes from his conflation of Ps 110:1 and Dan 7:13 with the implication that he is going to be enthroned with God.[103]

Again the high priest asked him, "Are you the Messiah, the Son of the Blessed One?""I am," said Jesus. "And you will see **the Son of Man** *sitting at the right* hand of the Mighty One and **coming on the clouds of heaven**." (Mark 14:61–62)	In my vision at night I looked, and there before me was one like a **son of man, coming with the clouds of heaven** (Dan 7:13) The LORD says to my lord: "*Sit at my right hand* until I make your enemies a footstool for your feet." (Ps 110:1)

The background to this saying and the explanation for why Jesus was thought to have committed blasphemy is the mooted question as to whether Yahweh shares his throne with another. In 3 En. 16 the sage Elisha ben Abuya had a vision of the angel Metatron on God's throne. Elisha claimed that there were "two powers in heaven," yet he was summarily rebuked by God himself. Similarly, there is the famous story of the great rabbi Akiba (died ca. 135 CE), who suggested that the plural "thrones" in Dan 7:9 included "one for God, one for David." His proposal was ap-

---

102. See Bird, *Are You the One Who Is to Come?* 136–40.

103. Kirk, *A Man Attested by God*, 329–30, is right that Jesus's opponents accuse him of blasphemy "for claiming to be God" but is wrong when he supposes that according to Mark "blasphemy is a charge levelled against those who fail to recognize that the spirit of God is the one at work in Jesus' authoritative ministry. . . . Blasphemy consists of a mocking denial of Jesus' Christological identity, put on display precisely by his going to death on the cross" (330). What Jesus's opponents regard as blasphemy, Mark regards as true—the gospel of Jesus Christ no less—and that is the dramatic christological irony of the Markan narrative!

parently met with a charge of blasphemy, to which Akiba is said to have capitulated.[104] Evidently, many Jews were allergic to the suggestion that Yahweh had a miniature throne buddy. Yet the Markan Jesus is interpreting Ps 110 and Dan 7:13–14 in a way that sees these texts as referring to his enthronement beside God. This builds upon and fills out what was asserted earlier in Jesus's exposition of Ps 110 in opposition to the scribes during his Jerusalem ministry that the Messiah, as David's κύριος, is also Yahweh's co-regent (Mark 12:35–37). The Markan Jesus's claim is not that he is going to sit on his own little throne next to God, but rather that he would sit at God's right hand on God's own throne. If Mark thinks that Dan 7:13–14 is about Jesus, then Mark is placing Jesus within the orbit of divine sovereignty and claiming a place for Jesus within the divine regency of "God Almighty." The imagery implies that Jesus will share in God's very own lordship.[105] The significance of this assertion is enormous, as Joshua Leim notes: "Not only does he claim to share in God's cosmic sovereignty by sitting on his throne, but also conflates that claim with the theophanic image of Daniel's Son of Man, exalted over his enemies, vindicated in his identity and mission."[106] What this means is that Caiaphas's question as to whether Jesus is the "Son of the Blessed One" is answered by way of reference to the Son of Man co-enthroned beside God and sharing in the visual marvel of the divine presence. In which case, as Boring states, "for Mark 'son of God' cannot be reduced to the Israelite idea that the king was adopted as God's son; instead it has an eschatological dimension related to the Son of Man."[107]

To come to a conclusion on Mark's divine Christology, we saw earlier that there is good evidence that the Markan Jesus should be regarded as the pre-existent Son on account of the acclamations of the demons who recognize him as the Son of God (Mark 1:24; 5:7) and that he transcends the heaven-earth divide as the Son of Man (Mark 8:38; 13:26; 14:62) and Son of God (Mark 13:32). He knows Moses and Elijah from a previous time and place (Mark 9:4), and Scripture records Yahweh addressing the Messiah as David's pre-existent Lord (Mark 12:35–37). In addition, it has been shown

104. *b. Hagigah* 14a; *b. Sanhedrin* 38b.
105. Joel Marcus, "Mark 14:61: 'Are You the Messiah-Son of God?'" *NovT* 31 (1989): 139.
106. Leim, "In the Glory of the Father," 230.
107. Boring, *Mark*, 251.

that (1) Mark's emphasis on monotheism includes the ambiguous identification of both God and Jesus as Israel's κύριος;[108] (2) The Markan Jesus exercises divine prerogatives in forgiving people of their sins; (3) Jesus's walking on the water and transfiguration contain theophanic qualities that make Jesus a virtual appearance of Yahweh; and (4) Jesus has divine authority as he is described not only as a member of the heavenly council but as one co-enthroned as Yahweh's vice-regent. On the whole, as Timothy Geddert has put it, the Markan Jesus is what only God can be, does what only God can do, and claims the allegiance that belongs only to the one true God.[109]

To synthesize the material surveyed above, we could proffer the following. The Markan Jesus participates in the kyriecentricity of Israel's God. He is identified as a pre-existent heavenly figure who has come to earth, who carries divine authority, who embodies a royal role; and in his person, words, and deeds he manifests the holy presence, the redemptive purposes, and the cosmic power of the Lord of Israel. In no case can Mark's Gospel—when read in light of its own context, claims, and its intertextuality—be said to describe Jesus as a human figure who becomes the divine son at some point in his career. I cannot put it any better than Boring: "It is . . . unMarkan to claim that Mark presents us with a human being Jesus who in the course of time is promoted to a higher ontological level, whether this be conceived as having happened at his baptism or at the resurrection/exaltation."[110]

Parallels and Markan Christology

One could potentially mute the evidence presented above for Mark mapping Jesus onto the divine identity by pointing to various parallels that

---

108. Leim, "In the Glory of the Father," 232, suggests the category of "divine-filial identity" to account for how Jesus's divine identity is determined and defined by a filial agency. He suggests that "This complex narration creates something of a *Verbindungsidentität* between the Father and the Son, a unity and differentiation, a sameness and Otherness." This is a proposal worth pondering.

109. Timothy J. Geddert, "The Implied YHWH Christology of Mark's Gospel: Mark's Challenge to the Readers to 'Connect the Dots,'" *BBR* 25 (2015): 7.

110. Boring, "Markan Christology," 471.

show human or angelic figures being attributed a similar range of prerogatives, powers, and status normally ascribed to Yahweh. This would show in effect that: (1) Mark's christological claims for Jesus are not unprecedented; (2) Jewish sources did not refrain from attributing divine prerogatives, powers, and status to human or angelic figures, as is often claimed; and (3) it might be better to describe Jesus as a divine agent than as a divine figure.

Several examples suffice to show what might be made of this point. On the authority to forgive sins, there is the Angel of the Lord, who can forgive (Exod 23:20–21; Zech 3:4). It is possible that a Jewish exorcist can forgive sins, according to the Qumran scrolls (4Q242 1–3.4, though the text is fragmentary, grammatically ambiguous, and the forgiver might be God). Jesus might be like Moses (Exod 32:31–32), Samuel (Josephus, *A.J.* 6.91–93), or certain conceptions of the Messiah (Tg. Isa. 53.4–12; CD 14.19, though again the text is fragmentary, grammatically ambiguous, and the forgiver could be God) in mediating divine forgiveness for the people. Having power over the sea and water is something that Yahweh does through human figures like Aaron and Moses (Ps 77:19–20). Israel's king is said to have authority over the rivers (Ps 89:25). God granted such authority over nature to Moses, according to Philo (*Mos.* 1.55–56). Philo also attributes such an authority to the Emperor Augustus (*Legat.* 145). Being transfigured with divine glory is something that was said to have been experienced by Moses (Exod 24:13–18; 34:29–35), and there are various Hellenistic metamorphosis stories, such as the transformation of the nurse Doso into the goddess Demeter (Homeric Hymn 2 to Demeter 275–80). Finally, figures like Moses (Ezek. Trag. 68–69) and Enoch (1 En. 48.5; 51.3; 55.4; 61.8; 62.2, 5; 69.27, 29; 71.14) were said to have been placed on either Yahweh's own throne or, like David (4Q504 4.6–8), put on a throne next to Yahweh.

These are all genuinely good points that warrant careful comparison with the Markan narrative. Even so, a couple of things can be said in response, not to reject the significance of these parallels, but to demonstrate that these parallels are more often than not analogues rather than explanations for Mark's depiction of Jesus as a divine figure.

(1) In many cases, I think the parallels are rather inexact. For instance, in Mark 2:1–12, Jesus does not offer to mediate divine forgiveness; rather,

he declares the forgiveness of sins on the back of his own unmediated authority. Concerning Jesus seated as God's viceroy, the heavenly enthronements of Moses (Ezek. Trag.) and Enoch (1 Enoch) are particularly interesting cases. However, Moses's enthronement is part of a dream sequence and merely underscores that he has Godlike authority over Israel as a superlative power and status. Enoch's enthronement seems to mean that he receives obeisance by all the inhabitants of the earth. Neither case constitutes an incursion into or sharing in Yahweh's divine authority. In contrast, in Mark 12:35–37 and 14:62, Jesus is depicted as one who sits on Yahweh's throne, the honorific position at the right hand of Israel's God. This is not his own little throne, but the same throne from which he exercises judgment. That is not to say that Mark's claims about Jesus are unprecedented or entirely unique, but the standard parallel texts cited here do not explain how or why Mark could attribute divine prerogatives and divine status to Jesus.

(2) In many cases there seems to be an assumption that there is a single "missing link" between Jewish theology and early Christology. Attempts are made by the study of parallel texts to discover this missing link, whether that is exalted patriarchs or angelic figures, who account for the shift from Jewish monotheism to christological monotheism. The problem is that there probably is no single link in the chain that explains the transition from Jewish monotheism to christological monotheism. It is far more probable, as Timo Eskola has argued, that the early church connected traditions that did not yet belong together in Second Temple Judaism.[111] This is evident in the clustering of Davidic messianism, resurrection, human ascent, angelomorphology, divine sonship, apocalyptic narratives, and reinterpreting YHWH-texts around Jesus, which blended a diverse array of Jewish types into a unique christological mosaic. While the presentation of Jesus as divine alongside Israel's God possesses clear continuity with Jewish types, the overall presentation, as traced among Mark or Paul or John, cannot be understood merely as the repackaging of any single set of Jewish types. Accordingly, the developing belief in Jesus's deity did not launch from any pre-existing package of parallel types, but emerged from the somewhat unique clustering of Jewish types that

111. Eskola, *Messiah and the Throne*, 383.

were freshly appropriated and reinterpreted in light of the experience and exegesis of the early church. The result, which is fairly consistent across the New Testament, is summed up by Eskola: "Christ is not merely an exalted patriarch, prophet, or pious king, whom God vindicated through exaltation. He is the Son of God, and faith in him realizes faith in the Lord of Israel."[112]

(3) Every generation of scholars needs to read Samuel Sandmel's warning against the perils of "parallelomania." Sandmel noted the "extravagance among scholars which first overdoes the supposed similarity in passages and then proceeds to describe source and derivation as if implying literary connection flowing in an inevitable or predetermined direction."[113] There is no question that Mark's Gospel needs to be understood in light of Second Temple Jewish and Greco-Roman literature. I have cited extra-biblical sources where I believe they illuminate or inform readers of Mark. Mark's Gospel is after all deeply intertextual and has manifold resonances with Jewish and Greco-Roman literary tropes and religious traditions that need to be explored. Such literature can illuminate Mark and illustrate the range of reasonable resonances that the Markan text might have with readers immersed in such literature and traditions. However, such parallelism becomes deeply problematic when the internal coherence and cumulative weight of Mark's narrative construction of Jesus's identity is nonchalantly set aside when an interpreter finds a parallel text and proceeds to argue to the effect that Mark's depiction of Jesus as A is really the same as the description of figure B in a parallel text. Even worse, there can be near endless multiplications of parallels with the result that the narration of the Markan Jesus doing/saying A becomes a debate over parallels B, C, D, or E. To give an example, the "meaning" of Mark 6:45–52, where Jesus walks on the water and calms the storm, cannot be resolved simply by piling up parallel texts like those which describe Yahweh with authority over the sea and stilling the storms (Job 9:8–11; Ps 107:23–30; Isa 43:16; 51:9–10; plus Exod 33:17–23 and 34:6 where Yahweh "passes by" Moses), or where Yahweh leads Israel through the sea by the hand of Moses and Aaron (Ps 77:19), or where Yahweh places the king in authority

---

112. Eskola, *Messiah and the Throne*, 390.
113. Samuel Sandmel, "Parallelomania," *JBL* 81 (1962): 1.

over the rivers (Ps 89:25). How does one adjudicate between these options as the primary parallel for accounting for Mark's presentation of Jesus?[114]

As a general rule, such parallel texts have interpretive value when the author has already cued the reader to expect a specific range of texts through citation, allusion, and echo; when the parallel texts fill in missing gaps in the narrative; when the parallel text enhances the overall coherence and main thrust of the story; or when the implied reader is expected to be familiar with the given text or tradition. Parallel texts create endless possibilities, but these possibilities are not probabilities, and mere possibilities do not explain the contours of the Markan story. The utility of the parallels must be assessed by how they enhance the internal consistency and narrative momentum of the Markan narrative. Without such a criterion the parallels do little more than become hermeneutical white noise and constitute a near endless list of possible associations that some readers might have made with some text in some location. Little is gained from this enterprise.

Conclusion

This chapter has attempted to demonstrate that Mark's Christology cannot be properly regarded as adoptionist. First, it is possible for a pagan reader immersed in the imperial cult with the deification of emperors to read the baptismal story as adoptionistic. Yet, one ought not read the baptismal scene this way when informed by Mark's wider literary context and intertextuality. Second, it was demonstrated that Mark's Christology as a whole cannot be played in an adoptionistic key because Mark portrays Jesus as a pre-existent figure with transcendent qualities who (ambiguously!) shares in the identity of Israel's κύριος.

---

114. Compare Hays, *Reading Backwards*, 24–28, and Daniel Kirk and Stephen L. Young, "I Will Set His Hand to the Sea: Psalm 86:28 (LXX) and Christology in Mark," *JBL* 133 (2014): 333–40. Fletcher-Louis, *Jesus Monotheism*, 130, who believes that christological monotheism has Jewish precedents, himself criticizes those who "take a minority or idiosyncratic position on possible examples of a precedent for some NT text or Christological theme. And . . . provide a brief discussion of a non-Christian text that leads to strong claims about its meaning and historical position where a fuller analysis would really be needed to sustain their case."

CHAPTER 5

How Jesus Got Adopted in the Second Century

So far this study has argued that there is no adoptionistic Christology extant in the New Testament. The texts normally assumed to contain an early adoptionism do not in fact represent an adoptionistic viewpoint (Rom 1:3–4; Acts 2:36; Mark 1:11). That does not prove that adoptionistic Christology did not exist in the first century CE, merely that our primary sources do not give evidence for its existence at this point. However, adoptionism did emerge at some point, and the question is precisely when? We thus now turn our attention to the second century and will look in particular at the likely suspects: the Shepherd of Hermas, the Ebionites, and the Theodotians.

The Shepherd and the Two Sons

The Shepherd of Hermas was a popular Christian writing that originated in Rome ca. 140 CE and is sometimes alleged to have an adoptionist Christology.[1] This is based on a mistaken reading of the fifth parable. In the

1. E.g., Alois Grillmeier and Theresia Hainthaler, *Jesus der Christus im Glauben der Kirche. I. Von der Apostolischen Zeit bis zum Konzil von Chalcedon (451)* (Freiburg im Breisgau: Herder, 1979), 159, who identifies in Herm. Sim. 5 a "distinctly adoptionistic Christology" ("Eine deutlich adoptianistische Christologie"), and Duane Olson, *Issues in Contemporary Christian Thought: A Fortress Introduction* (Minneapolis: Fortress, 2011), 87, says adoptionism "was the positon of a popular Christian writing from the

parable there is the story of a servant who fences and diligently tends to his master's vineyard and after is rewarded for his good work by being made a fellow heir with the master's son (Herm. Sim. 5.2.6–8). Later in the explanation of the parable (Herm. Sim. 5.5.2), according to some witnesses, we read that "the Son is the Holy Spirit" (ὁ δὲ υἱὸς τὸ πνεῦμα τὸ ἅγιόν ἐστιν), in contrast to the "servant" who "is the Son of God" (ὁ δὲ δοῦλος ὁ υἱὸς τοῦ θεοῦ ἐστιν). Taken together, it would imply that the servant (i.e., Jesus) was adopted with the Son (i.e., Holy Spirit) as a reward for his obedience to God.

[5.2.1] Listen to the parable which I am about to tell you which relates to fasting. [2] A certain man had a field and many slaves. And on a certain part of the field he planted a vineyard. And choosing a certain faithful, pleasing, and honored slave, he called him and said to him, "Take this vineyard which I planted and fence it until I come, and do not do otherwise to the vineyard. And keep this commandment of mine and you will gain freedom from me." And the master of the slave went out on his journey. [3] And when he had gone, the servant took and fenced in the vineyard. And finishing the fencing in of the vineyard, he saw that the vineyard was full of weeds. [4] Therefore he reasoned in himself, saying, "This commandment of the master I have accomplished, next I will cultivate this vineyard and it will look even better after cultivation. And not having weeds, it will produce even more fruit, not being choked by the weeds." After taking it, he cultivated the vineyard and all the weeds which were in the vineyard, he pulled them out. And that vineyard was looking its best and thriving, not having weeds choking it. [5] After some time, the master of the slave and of the field came. And he entered into the vineyard and upon seeing the vineyard attractively fenced in, and in addition also cultivated and all the weeds pulled out and the vines were thriving, he rejoiced greatly because of the work of

early or mid-second century called *Shepherd of Hermas*." Caroline Osiek, *The Shepherd of Hermas*, Hermeneia (Minneapolis: Fortress, 1999), 179–81, is more cautious in noting the ambiguity that some elements like 5.6.7 make a strictly adoptionist interpretation "impossible," while the overall impression is more accurately "monotheistic with preexistence (but not necessarily divine) spirit and exalted Son of God." She adds: "Trinitarian in the orthodox sense it certainly is not."

the servant. ⁶ *Therefore calling his beloved son, who was his heir and his friends who were counselors, he said to them what he commanded to his servant and what he found accomplished, and those people rejoiced with the servant because of the testimony which the master testified to him. ⁷ And he said to them, "I promised freedom to this servant if he might keep my commandment which I commanded to him. And he kept my commandment and added good work to the vineyard, and I was exceedingly pleased. Therefore because of this work which he has done, I want to make him a fellow heir with my son, because the good which he thought to do he did not disregard but accomplished it." ⁸ The son of the master agreed with this his intention, that the slave might become a fellow heir with the son.* ⁹ After a few days, he made a feast and sent much food to him from the feast. But the servant, after receiving the food which was sent to him from the master, kept what was sufficient for him and distributed the rest to his fellow servants. ¹⁰ And his fellow servants, after receiving the food, rejoiced and began to pray for him, that he might find greater favor from the master because he had treated them in this way. ¹¹ All these things that happened, his master heard and again rejoiced exceedingly because of his action. The master, again summoning his friends and his son, reported to them his deed, that he did with his food which he received. *And they were in even more agreement that the slave should become a fellow heir with his son.*

^{5.5.1} "I told you," he said, "even now, that you are crafty and arrogant, asking for the explanations of the parables. But since you are so persistent, I will explain to you the parable of the field and the rest of all that follows, that you may make them known to everyone. Listen now," he said, "and understand them. ² *The field is this world, and the master of the field is the one who created all things and perfected and strengthened them. [And the Son is the Holy Spirit] and the servant is the Son of God, and the vines are this people which he himself planted. ³ And the fences are the holy angels of the Lord who support his people. And the weeds which were pulled out from the vineyard are lawless deeds of the servants of God. And the food which was sent to him from the feast are the commandments which he gave to his people through his Son, and the friends and counselors are the holy angels who were first created. And the absence of the master is the time*

which remains until his coming. ⁴ I said to him, "Sir, all is great and wonderful, and all is glorious. How, then," I said, "could I have understood these things? Nor [anyone else], even if extremely intelligent, [no one would] be able to understand them. Yet," I said, "sir, explain to me what I am about to ask you." ⁵ "Speak," he said, "if you want something." "Why," I said, "sir, does the Son of God appear in the guise of a servant in the parable?"

⁵·⁶·¹ "Listen," he said, "The *Son of God* does not appear in the guise of a servant, but appears in great power and lordship." "How," I said, "sir? I do not understand." ² "Because," he said, "God planted the vineyard, that is, he created the people, and gave it over to his *Son*. And the *Son* appointed the angels over them to preserve them, and he himself purified their sin, laboring much and enduring much toil. For no vineyard is able to be cultivated apart from toil or hardship. ³ *Therefore he, having purified the sins of the people, he made known to them the well-worn paths of life, giving them the law which he received from his Father.* ⁴ ["You see," he said, "that He is the Lord of the people, having received all authority from his Father.] *But why did the Lord take his Son and the glorious angels as counselor concerning the inheritance of the servant? Listen.* ⁵ *The Holy Spirit, which pre-exists, which created all creation, God caused to dwell in the flesh that he desired. Therefore this flesh in which the Holy Spirit dwelled served the Spirit well, walking in holiness and purity, in no way at all defiling the Spirit.* ⁶ *Therefore it, having lived commendably and purely, and having labored together with the Spirit and having worked together in all deeds, behaving strongly and bravely, he took it as partner with the Holy Spirit. For the conduct of this flesh pleased him because it was not defiled upon the earth while possessing the Holy Spirit.* ⁷ *Therefore he took the Son and the glorious angels as counselor, that this flesh also, having served the Spirit blamelessly, might have some dwelling place, and not seem to have lost the reward of its service. For all flesh will receive a reward, the flesh found undefiled and without fault, in which the Holy Spirit has dwelt.* ⁸ *You also have the explanation of this parable.*"²

2. Herm. Sim. 5.2.1–5.6.8 (Brannan, Lexham).

On a close reading, there are several factors that tell against an adoptionist reading of the parable:

(1) There is a clear statement of the Son of God's pre-existence elsewhere in the Shepherd of Hermas: "The Son of God is older than all of his creation, so that he was counselor to the Father of his creation" (Herm. Sim. 9.12.2), and the Son of God is described in angelic language in many places (Herm. Vis. 5.2; Herm. Sim. 5.4.4; 7.1–3, 5; esp. Herm. Sim. 8.3.3, 9.1.3, 9.12.7–8).

(2) The main point of the fifth parable is that upright conduct is eminently superior to fasting, so the purpose of the parable is soteriological rather than christological. Jesus's flesh attained immortality by his righteousness and this is an example for others to emulate (Herm. Sim. 5.1.1–4; 5.7.1–2). The possibility of the servant becoming a co-heir with the master's son is merely a metaphor for reward rather than a mode of the servant's actual metamorphosis: "For all flesh will receive a reward, the flesh found undefiled and without fault, in which the Holy Spirit has dwelt" (Herm. Sim. 5.6.7).

(3) In the parable, the "servant" does not become the master's "son" only an "heir." While sons would normally be heirs, not all heirs had to become sons. Heirs could be established without adoption. Peppard notes that "the parable is careful not to call the slave a son, even after he has been granted inheritance."[3]

(4) The fact that the Son of God receives "power and lordship" (Herm. Sim. 5.6.1) and (in the longer reading) "all authority from the Father" (Herm. Sim. 5.6.4) is not adoptionist any more than Matt 28:18, where the risen Jesus says, "All authority in heaven and on earth has been given to me."

The Christology of the Shepherd of Hermas is complicated and even incoherent. It shows that not everyone was on the road to Nicea. However, it would be unwise to categorize the Shepherd of Hermas as an adoptionistic text. The fifth parable is particularly confusing as the identity of the "Son" and "Son of God" is not always clear. Even so, its primary point is the eschatological reward for a blameless life. Peppard is correct that the parable is not adoptionist but exaltationist and exemplarist.[4] Yet, to that

---

3. Peppard, *Son of God*, 235n102.
4. Peppard, *Son of God*, 152.

we need to add a wider picture of the christological claims of the Shepherd of Hermas, where the Spirit and Son are in effect conflated (Herm. Sim. 9.1.1), and the one thing they share is pre-existence (Herm. Sim. 5.6.5; 9.12.2). What is more, the Shepherd of Hermas has something very akin to an angel-Christology.[5] So, if the Son of God is conflated with the Spirit and equated in some way with an archangel like Michael, then he is somewhere between an incarnation of the Holy Spirit and an anthropophany of the archangel Michael. Thus, it is better to speak of a Christology of pre-existence and exaltation in the Shepherd of Hermas.

The Ebionites: Poor Man's Christology

The Ebionites were a Jewish Christian group whose origins are shrouded in mystery. Everything about the group, including their sacred texts and beliefs, is contested.[6] The problem is that our sources about the Ebionites are scant and come exclusively from their Gentile Christian critics. We should be cautious in accepting the words of western writers who may not have met any eastern Jewish Christians in their lifetimes and simply recycled caricatures and critiques of previous authors. Even worse, while Jewish Christianity was diverse, with orthodox and heterodox varieties,[7]

---

5. In fact, Tertullian, *Carn. Chr.* 14, critiques an angel-Christology that seems straight out of the Shepherd of Hermas's fifth parable given the mention of a Lord, vineyard, son, servant, and angels.

6. For an introduction, see Albertus F. J Klijn and G. J. Reinink, *Patristic Evidence for Jewish-Christian Sects*, NovTSup 36 (Leiden: Brill, 1973), 19–43; Richard Bauckham, "The Origin of the Ebionites," in *The Image of the Judaeo-Christians in Ancient Jewish and Christian Literature*, ed. Peter J. Tomson and Doris Lambers-Petry, WUNT 158 (Tübingen: Mohr Siebeck, 2003), 162–81; Sakari Häkkinen, "Ebionites," in *A Companion to Second-Century Christian "Heretics,"* ed. Antti Marjanen and Petri Luomanen, VCSup 76 (Leiden: Brill, 2005), 247–78; Oskar Skarsaune, "The Ebionites," in *Jewish Believers in Jesus*, ed. Oskar Skarsaune and Reidar Hvalvik (Peabody, MA: Hendrickson, 2007), 419–62; David E. Wilhite, *The Gospel according to Heretics: Discovering Orthodoxy through Early Christological Conflicts* (Grand Rapids: Baker, 2015), esp. ch. 2; Papandrea, *Earliest Christologies*, 23–43.

7. See Justin, *Dial.* 46–48, on Jewish Christians with a Christology approximate to his own; Origen, *Cels.* 5.61, regarded some Ebionites as orthodox on Jesus's virgin birth but merely following a Jewish way of life; and Jerome, *Comm. Isa.* 8.11–15, 19–22; 11.1–3, 17.17–21, on the Nazarenes, whom he regarded as observant Jewish believers in Jesus.

eventually some authors seem to have regarded all or any Jewish Christians as Ebionites. Notwithstanding such caveats, many scholars still remain confident that this group held adoptionistic beliefs. For instance, Ehrman describes the Ebionites as a group of Jewish Christians living east of the Jordan who "maintained that Jesus was a remarkable man . . . chosen by God to be his son . . . 'adopted' at his baptism."[8] For many scholars it is indeed ironic that the Ebionites were later rejected as heretics for holding to what was the earliest interpretation of Jesus: that he was a man adopted by God at his baptism.[9] However, as we will see, this may not actually be the case. The claim that the Ebionites were adoptionists is not certain.[10] It is far more likely that they held something tantamount to a "possession" Christology.

The Ebionites were said to have emerged from the band of Jewish Christians who fled Jerusalem and made for Pella at the outbreak of the Jewish war in the late 60s CE and owe their direction to a teacher called "Ebion."[11] While the tradition of the flight of Jewish Christians to Pella is probably correct,[12] whether the Ebionites trace their origins to this group is moot because most groups claimed lineage from the apostles. The existence of an actual figure called "Ebion" is unlikely since the name Ebion derives from the Hebrew *'ebyon* for "poor" and to name a son *Ebion* would be tantamount to the naming him "Pauper." Most likely the name *ebionites* emerged from

8. Bart D. Ehrman, *The New Testament: A Historical Introduction to the Early Christian Writings*, 4th ed. (Oxford: Oxford University Press, 2008), 3; Bart D. Ehrman, *Lost Christianities: The Battles for Scripture and the Faiths We Never Knew* (Oxford: Oxford University Press, 2003), 99–103; Ehrman, *How Jesus Became God*, 290–91.

9. Dunn, *Unity and Diversity in the New Testament*, 242; Dunn, *Christology in the Making*, 33–36.

10. I share the frustration of Charles E. Hill, "An Exclusive Religion: Orthodoxy and Heresy, Inclusion and Exclusion," in *How God Became Jesus: The Real Origins of Belief in Jesus' Divine Nature*, ed. Michael F. Bird (Grand Rapids: Zondervan, 2014), 161: "Our earliest reports of a group known as Ebionites never say that they believed Jesus had been exalted to divine status. Ever. Not at his resurrection (supposedly the view of the earliest Christians), nor at his baptism (supposedly the view of the gospel of Mark), nor at his birth (supposedly the view of the gospels of Matthew and Luke)."

11. Epiphanius, *Pan.* 30.2.7–8, following Eusebius, *Hist. eccl.* 3.5.

12. See the review of the debate and the positive appraisal of the historicity of the Pella tradition in Victoria Balabanski, *Eschatology in the Making: Mark, Matthew and the Didache*, SNTSMS 97 (Cambridge: Cambridge University Press, 2005), 100–135.

a Jewish Christian group who relied on Jewish (Pss 9–10, 12, 14, 37, 113; Isa 61:1; 4Q171 2.9, 3.10), Jesus (Matt 5:7/Luke 6:20), or apostolic (Rom 15:26; Gal 2:9; Jas 2:5) tradition to identify themselves as poor and humble before God.[13] Early heresiologists wrongly inferred from this name that a teacher called "Ebion" must have been the originator of the group[14] since all heresies were explained by genealogy.[15] The Ebionites were remembered and renounced in patristic tradition as a deviant Jewish Christian group who followed the Jewish way of life, disavowed Paul, relied almost entirely on the Gospel of Matthew, and rejected the virgin birth. Jerome did not mince his words saying that they wanted to be both Jews and Christians, but were regarded by both rabbis and bishops as "neither Jews nor Christians" deriving from "Ebion that arch-heretic, half-Christian and half-Jew."[16]

The earliest summary of their teaching comes to us from Irenaeus, who may have been relying on either Justin's *Syntagma* or perhaps an updated version of it:[17]

> Those who are called Ebionites agree that the world was made by God; but their opinions with respect to the Lord are similar[18] to those of Cerinthus and Carpocrates. They use the Gospel according to Matthew

13. Some used the wordplay on "poor" against them, saying their name is indicative of their "poor understanding": "The ancients quite properly called these men Ebionites, because they held poor and mean opinions concerning Christ" (McGiffert, *NPNF*²; Eusebius, *Hist. eccl.* 3.27.1, 6; cf. Eusebius, *Hist. eccl.* 1.14; Origen, *Cels.* 2.1; Epiphanius, *Pan.* 30.17.1–2; 30.18.1; Jerome, *Comm. Isa.* 1.3).

14. Tertullian, *Praes. Haer.* 33; Epiphanius, *Pan.* 30.1.1.

15. Justin, *Dial.* 35.6, wrote: "Some are called Marcians, and some Valentinians, and some Basilidians, and some Saturnilians, and others by other names; each called after the originator of the individual opinion, just as each one of those who consider themselves philosophers, as I said before, thinks he must bear the name of the philosophy which he follows, from the name of the father of the particular doctrine" (Coxe, *ANF*).

16. Jerome, *Epist.* 112.13; *Comm. Gal.* 3.13–14; *Comm. Isa.* 2.22.

17. Häkkinen, "Ebionites," 250–51.

18. In some witnesses to the Latin text it says "not similar," whereas when Hippolytus quotes this passage from Irenaeus it has no negation. Klijn and Reinink, *Patristic Evidence for Non-Jewish Sects*, 19–20, think the negation should be included, but more compelling is Skarsaune, "The Ebionites," 428, who excludes it because if the Ebionites were not similar to Cerinthus and Carpocrates. If that is the case, then there is no reason for Irenaeus to include them at this point.

only, and repudiate the Apostle Paul, maintaining that he was an apostate from the law. As to the prophetical writings, they endeavour to expound them in a somewhat singular manner: they practise circumcision, persevere in the observance of those customs which are enjoined by the law, and are so Judaic in their style of life, that they even adore Jerusalem as if it were the house of God.[19]

Our picture, however, is complicated, as there were several varieties of Ebionism. Some Ebionites reportedly rejected the virgin conception,[20] while others accepted it,[21] which indicates varying viewpoints on Jesus's pre-existence, divinity, and humanity. It is also said that they believed that Jesus was a mere man justified or elected on account of his superior virtue.[22] Furthermore, among the Jewish Christian Gospels, there is a so-called Gospel of the Ebionites cited by Epiphanius, most likely a Gospel harmony based largely on Matthew.[23] This Gospel includes an account of Jesus's baptism with a full citation of Ps 2:7 in the divine voice ("Today, I have begotten you"), plus adding details about a great light that shone all around and a more embellished account of John the Baptist's response.[24]

---

19. Irenaeus, *Adv. Haer.* 1.26.2 (Roberts and Rambaut, *ANF*); see 3.11.7; 3.21.1; 4.33.4; 5.1.3. On the authenticity of Irenaeus's description, see Michael D. Goulder, "A Poor Man's Christology," *NTS* 45 (1999): 335–37; and James Carleton Paget, "Jewish Christianity," in *Cambridge History of Judaism*, ed. William Horbury, W. D. Davies, and John Sturdy, 3 vols. (Cambridge: Cambridge University Press, 2001), 757.

20. Irenaeus, *Adv. Haer.* 5.1.3; Tertullian, *Virg.* 6.1; Eusebius, *Hist. Eccl.* 3.27.2; 5.8.10; 6.17; Epiphanius, *Pan.* 30.2.1–2; 30.3.1; Origen, *Hom. Luc* 17; *Cels.* 5.61.

21. Eusebius, *Hist. Eccl.* 3.27.3; Origen, *Comm. Matt.* 16.12; *Cels.* 5.61.

22. Hippolytus, *Haer.* 7.22, stresses also the exemplary nature of Jesus for the Ebionites: "And the Ebionæans allege that they themselves also, when in like manner they fulfil the law, are able to become Christs; for they assert that our Lord Himself was a man in a like sense with all the rest of the human family" (MacMahon, *ANF*). Similar is Eusebius, *Hist. Eccl.* 3.27.2: "they held him to be a plain and ordinary man, who had achieved righteousness merely by the progress of his character" (Lake, *LCL*); and Epiphanius, *Pan.* 30.18.6: "Christ alone, they would have it, is prophet, man, Son of God, and Christ—and as I said before he is a mere man who has come to be called Son of God owing to the virtue of his life" (Williams).

23. Of course, whether this Gospel was produced or used by the Ebionites cannot be guaranteed, see Skarsaune, "The Ebionites," 457–61.

24. Gos. Eb. 4.

Even after his baptism, when Jesus enters Capernaum, he is described in very human terms; no massive transformation appears to have occurred: "There was a certain man named Jesus, who was about thirty years old. He is the one who chose us [disciples]."[25] Yet the same Gospel of the Ebionites is alleged to have recorded that Jesus was not from God the Father, but created as one of the archangels, made to rule over the lesser angels and over all of creation.[26] Tertullian records a similar dichotomy in Ebionite Christology, in which Jesus is a mere human and not the Son of God, but more properly an angelic being in human form. Tertullian alleges that Ebion "holds Jesus to be a mere man, and nothing more than a descendant of David, and not also the Son of God; although He is, to be sure, in one respect more glorious than the prophets, inasmuch as he declares that there was an angel in Him, just as there was in Zechariah."[27]

Epiphanius provides a synthesis and supplement to patristic heresiologies about the Ebionites, writing against the Christology of the Ebionites no less than four times.[28] The first account focuses on Jesus as a pre-existent spirit, ranked above the angels, ruler over them, and who appeared to the patriarchs. In the last days he put on Adam's body, appeared to men, was crucified, rose, and ascended.[29] Second, Christ is a divine being sent from God, who descended in the form of a dove into the man Jesus, who himself was born of human procreation.[30] Third, "Jesus was begotten of the seed of a man and chosen, and thus has been named Son of God by election [ἐκλογὴν υἱόν θεοῦ κληθέντα], after Christ who came to him from on high in the form of a dove."[31] Fourth, "Christ is prophet of truth and Christ; [but] that he is Son of God by promotion [υἱόν θεοῦ κατὰ

25. Gos. Eb. 5 (Ehrman and Pleše).
26. Gos. Eb. 7.
27. Tertullian, Carn. Chr. 14 (Holmes, ANF); cf. Praes. Haer. 33.11.
28. Epiphanius is also the most problematic of sources. He is obviously dependent on earlier heresiologists yet he claims to have first-hand experience with the Ebionites in Cyprus. Epiphanius believes that there was a real person called Ebion (which is doubted by most), who even visited Rome. The Ebionites were influenced by the false prophet Elaxai, and much of what Epiphanius attributes to the Ebionites is probably lifted out of the Pseudo-Clementine literature.
29. Epiphanius, Pan. 30.3.3–6.
30. Epiphanius, Pan. 30.14.4.
31. Epiphanius, Pan. 30.16.3 (Williams).

προκοπὴν], and by his connection with the elevation given to him from above [καὶ συνάφειαν ἀναγωγῆς τῆς ἄνωθεν πρὸς αὐτὸν γεγενημένης] . . . He alone, they would have it, is a prophet, man, Son of God, and Christ— and yet a mere man, as I said, though owing to virtue of life he has come to be called the Son of God [διὰ δὲ ἀρετὴν βίου ἥκοντα εἰς τὸ καλεῖσθαι υἱόν θεοῦ]."[32] Epiphanius provides an eclectic set of descriptors majoring on a separation of the angelic "Christ" from the man "Jesus," and when the two are joined together the subject is elevated to the status of "Son of God."

All of this should indicate that there are substantial problems in identifying the Ebionites as adoptionists.

(1) There is the problem of sources. The paucity of sources and partiality of patristic authors is such that, as Peppard notes, "we do not know enough about the Ebionites to assess their imagery and metaphors of divine sonship."[33] On top of that, the Ebionites are said to have been diverse among themselves. A multiplicity of christological positions are claimed for the Ebionites.[34] As a result, it is impossible to envisage a single Christology for them. Evidence from patristic comments and Gospel fragments gives the impression that some of the Ebionites *might* have held to adoptionism, or angel-Christology, or possession Christology or a mixture of all of these.

(2) If adoptionism originated as a deliberate analogizing of Christ's status from Roman adoption practices, then it makes sense that the groups who would be most likely to gravitate toward adoptionist interpretations of Jesus would be those living in an immediate Roman provenance rather than among Jewish groups living in the Trans-Jordan. The cities in the Trans-Jordan were long Hellenized, under Roman hegemony, and populated with Jewish inhabitants, as well as Syrians, Arabs, and Parthians. It was a Roman territory, but not culturally Romanized like Corinth or Philippi. So we should not expect Roman adoption practices to be the germinal seeds for Jewish Christian Christology. That makes all the more sense when we remember that political adoptions were not normally practiced in Palestine.[35]

---

32. Epiphanius, *Pan.* 30.18.5–6 (Williams).
33. Peppard, *Son of God*, 147.
34. See esp. Epiphanius, *Pan.* 30.34.6.
35. Weiss, *Earliest Christianity*, 1:118 n. 70, acknowledges this point, but simply ignores what it means for his attempt to plant the origins of Christology in Jewish soil.

(3) The Gospel of the Ebionites includes an embellished account of Jesus's baptism and an extended citation of Ps 2:7, yet that no more indicates an adoptionist Christology than it does for Justin Martyr, who also had an embellished narration of Jesus's baptism and a full citation of Ps 2:7, including the words "Today I have begotten you."[36] Peppard points out that a better candidate for a baptismal adoption among the apocryphal Gospels might be the Gospel of the Hebrews as quoted by Jerome: "And it came to pass when the Lord came up out of the water, the whole fount of the Holy Spirit descended upon him and rested on him and said to him: 'My Son, in all the prophets I was waiting for you that you should come and I might rest in you. For you are my rest; you are my first-begotten Son that reigns forever."[37] Although this might be a better candidate for a baptismal adoption the problem is, as Peppard goes on to comment, "the imagery is actually more Johannine: it is a begetting again from above, as corroborated later by the Gospels' construal of the Holy Spirit as Jesus's 'mother.'"[38] In light of this my maxim would be: a baptism and a divine voice that says "my Son" does not an adoption make. This goes to show that stricter criteria for adoptionism are required that explicitly describe Jesus as moving from a state of non-sonship to divine sonship.

(4) It is with the descriptions from Epiphanius that we come the closest to adoptionist language attributed to the Ebionites. Jesus becomes the Son of God as a reward for his virtuous life. Yet the language we find is that of election (ἐκλογή), promotion (προκοπή), elevation (ἀναφέρω), and calling (καλέω). There is no explicit reference to adoption (υἱοθεσία) in any instance. The man Jesus is certainly given an exalted status as Son of God. Yet there is no indication that this exaltation has associations with kingship or a fictive filial relationship with Israel's God, which is normally associated with Son of God discourse in Christian texts. Moreover, Tertullian strangely claims that the Ebionites denied that Jesus was the Son of God. This could be a denial of pre-existent divine sonship, or simply indicate that after two unsuccessful Jewish revolts that were buoyed on by messianic claimants, the Ebionites were done with messianism as a cate-

---

36. See Luke 3:22 according to Codex Bezae (D); Gos. Eb. 4; Justin, *Dial.* 88, 103, and the discussion in Peppard, *Son of God*, 147.

37. Jerome, *Comm. Isa.* 11.1–3.

38. Peppard, *Son of God*, 234n82.

gory for a redeeming figure. In any case, the language used by Epiphanius to describe the beliefs of the Ebionites more properly denotes *exaltation*, though the title "Son of God" might connote *adoption*.

(5) A more interesting proposal is the connection that Irenaeus makes between the Ebionites, Carpocrates, and Cerinthus.[39] Reconstructing these two teachers and their followers represents a particular set of problems. Once again, we rely on second-hand accounts that assume a genetic relationship between these figures. There was a propensity to paint all dissidents with the same brush. Yet the one thing that seems to connect the trio of Carpocrates, Cerinthus, and Ebion(ites) together is the belief that a separate power, person, Christ, angel, spirit, or aeon entered into the man Jesus. While Irenaeus does not explicitly mention the Ebionites as holding to a possession Christology, it resonates with what is attributed to them in other patristic accounts that we have seen.[40] If this is the case, then the best label to describe the Ebionite belief is not adoptionism, but a possession Christology: a heavenly power or angel entered into the man Jesus. He then became the exalted Son of God.[41]

On the origins of the Ebionites, Bauckham comments: "It is even possible that the first Ebionites were Jews who had come to believe that Jesus was the Messiah but found the exalted Christological claims made for him by other Christians unacceptable."[42] What they found objectionable can be discerned from what seems to have distinguished their Christology from others: they objected to incarnationalism as an affront to monotheism

---

39. Irenaeus, *Adv. Haer.* 1.26.2.

40. Tertullian, *Carn. Chr.* 14; Ps-Tertullian, *Haer.* 3; Hippolytus, *Ref.* 7.22; 10.18; Epiphanius, *Pan.* 30.1.3; 30.3.4–6; 30.14.4; 30.34.6.

41. Alan Segal, "Jewish Christianity," in *Eusebius, Christianity, and Judaism*, ed. Harold W. Attridge and Gōhei Hata (Detroit: Wayne State University, 1992), 342–46, goes so far as to associate the Ebionites with the "two powers in heaven" heresy known to the rabbis. Eskola, *Messiah and the Throne*, 302, 307, 382, says that: "The distinguishing feature [of the Ebionites according to Irenaeus] is precisely the idea that Christ has descended on Jesus." Eskola explains, "In Ebionite interpretation Jesus is possessed by an angelic Christ" (307). Eskola concludes "Ebionite theology has appeared to be dualistic Gnostic possessionism which has nothing in common with New Testament Christology, but which is rather related to the so-called Sethian Gnosticism, well known in extant writings" (382).

42. Bauckham, "Origin of the Ebionites," 175.

and an endangerment to the humanity of Jesus. Although there were undoubtedly variations among their circle, they can be generally described as holding to a possession Christology with traces of angel-Christology. At most, adoptionism might be an implicit or loose connotation.[43] What is clear is that the old and repeated claim that the Ebionites were a single Jewish Christian group with an adoptionist Christology is patently false.[44]

Theodotus of Byzantium: Jesus Finally Gets Adopted

"As a distinct heresy," says Harold Brown, "adoptionism did not make its appearance until about the year 190 in Rome, where it was certainly partly a reaction against the gnostic speculation that made of Christ an immaterial aeon."[45] The idea is associated with Theodotus of Byzantium, a leatherworker or cobbler, who came to Rome.[46] Critics alleged that Theodotus had denied the faith while in Byzantium and fled to Rome. When confronted with his denial, he responded that he had only denied a mere man, not God.[47] However, it is more likely that his views were carefully articulated rather than an improvised excuse for his apostasy.[48] He was excommunicated by Bishop Victor of Rome before the end of the second century.[49]

Theodotus's scheme accepted orthodox views of God and creation, perhaps holding to the virgin birth.[50] The crux was that Jesus was a "mere man" (ψιλὸς ἄνθρωπος) who was supremely virtuous. Thereafter, the Spirit or Christ descended upon him at his baptism, enabling him to perform miracles.[51] Theodotus is said to have emphasized certain texts like

43. Papandrea, *Earliest Christologies*, 21, thinks these should be combined together and he labels it "Angel Adoptionism."
44. Cf. similarly Eskola, *Messiah and the Throne*, 305, 308–9.
45. Harold O. J. Brown, *Heresies* (New York: Doubleday, 1984), 96.
46. Hippolytus, *Refut.* 7.23; 10.19; Eusebius, *Hist. Eccl.* 5.28.6; Epiphanius, *Pan.* 54.1.3.
47. Epiphanius, *Pan.* 54.1.5–6.
48. Kelly, *Early Christian Doctrines*, 116.
49. Eusebius, *Hist. Eccl.* 5.28.9.
50. According to Hippolytus, *Refut.* 7.23; 10.19, though Epiphanius, *Pan.* 54.1.8, 54.3.2–4, 12, 54.6.4, implies that he denied the virgin birth.
51. Hippolytus, *Refut.* 7.23; 10.19; Eusebius, *Hist. Eccl.* 5.28.6; Epiphanius, *Pan.* 54.1.8.

Deut 18:15, Isa 53:3–8, and Jer 17:8, in which God promised to raise up a human prophet in the future.[52] He summarized the apostolic testimony to Jesus with the description of Jesus as "a man approved by signs and wonders" (Acts 2:22) and the "one mediator between God and man the man Christ Jesus" (1 Tim 2:5).[53] Hippolytus reports diversity among the Theodotians, "But among them some do not consider that Christ became divine, even at the descent of the Spirit; while others consider that he was made God after his resurrection from the dead" (θεὸν δὲ οὐδέποτε τὸν χριστὸν γεγονέναι αὐτός θέλει < τῶν δὲ ἀπ᾽ αὐτοῦ τινὲς μὲν > ἐπὶ τῇ καθόδῳ τοῦ πνεύματος, ἕτεροι δὲ μετὰ τὴν ἐκ νεκρῶν < αὐτοῦ > ἀνάστασιν).[54] Theodotus's followers interpreted the Scriptures in philosophical fashion. They were influenced by the philosophies of Euclid, Aristotle, Theophrastus, and Galen, and are alleged to have tinkered with biblical texts.[55] Theodotians are said to have articulated their positions as syllogisms. Theodotus the leatherworker had his views taken up by Theodotus the banker, Asclepiodotus, and Artemas, who fused this view of Jesus as a mere man with speculations about Melchizedek, whom they regarded as "the supreme Power," superior even to the heavenly Christ. Melchizedek is the "Son of God" who appeared to Abraham and is "an archon of righteousness ordained in heaven by God for this very purpose, a spiritual being and appointed to God's priesthood."[56] Christ bore a likeness to this Melchizedek, so that the heavenly Christ is a being who came upon the man Jesus at his baptism.[57] In which case, the man Jesus was anointed by God and made his elect one to turn people from idols and to show them the way of God.[58]

52. Epiphanius, *Pan.* 54.3.1; 54.4.1–5.4.
53. Epiphanius, *Pan.* 54.5.9.
54. Hippolytus, *Refut.* 7.23 (my own trans.); 10.19.
55. Eusebius, *Hist. Eccl.* 5.28.13–19.
56. Epiphanius, *Pan.* 55.7.3; 55.8.1 (F. Williams). See the Nag Hammadi Codices on Melchizedek 25.4–26.4 that equates Jesus with Melchizedek: "And you crucified me from the third hour of the Sabbath-eve until the ninth hour. And after these things, I arose from the dead, [. . .] came out of [. . .] into me, [. . .] my eyes saw [. . .], they did not find anyone . . . . . . greeted me [. . .]. They said to me, 'Be strong, O Melchizedek, great High-priest of God Most High'" (Pearson and Giversen).
57. Hippolytus, *Refut.* 7.24; Epiphanius, *Pan.* 55.1.1–5; 55.4.1.
58. Epiphanius, *Pan.* 55.8.3.

Going on the sources that we have here, even Theodotus the leather-worker cannot be properly called an adoptionist.[59] Theodotus believed that Jesus was a mere man, who received Christ or the Spirit at his baptism, and, according to Hippolytus, our earliest source on him, he never claimed that Jesus was divine or became divine in any sense. He saw Jesus exclusively as a Spirit-empowered prophet and nothing more, as far as our sources tell us. Among the Theodotians there was a mixture of beliefs that brought together views of Jesus a mere man (from Theodotus), a possession Christology (Cerinthus), something akin to the "two powers in heaven" heresy (known to the rabbis), and speculations on Melchizedek (known at Qumran, perhaps reflected in Hebrews, and attested in the Nag Hammadi Codices). One group of the Theodotians, who held that Jesus was deified after his resurrection, were the first, true, authentic, and genuine adoptionists, as far as definitions and evidence go. I speculate that these Theodotians were perhaps inspired to their Christology by the deifications of the emperors Pertinax (193 CE), Commodus (belatedly, 197 CE), and Septimius Severus (211 CE) around this time.[60] And perhaps they took direct influence from Galen, who "talks about a number of gods, yet at the same time seems to believe in a divine demiurge who has all the hallmarks of a monotheistic god."[61] And that finally settles how, when, and who first saw Jesus as a human adopted to divine sonship: it occurred sometime in the 190s or early 200s, in Rome, through a group of Theodotians.

59. Contra Ehrman, *Lost Christianities*, 152–53, who summarizes: "Theodotus maintained that Jesus was a 'mere man,' born of the sexual union of Joseph and Mary, but chosen by God at his baptism to be the savior of the world" and later calls him and his followers "Roman 'adoptionists.'"

60. Dio Cassius, *Hist.* 75.4.1–75.5.6; Herodion, 2.10.9; 4.2.1–11. Peppard, *Son of God*, 147, comments about them: "But we can say that the adoptive imagery of the Theodotians would have been especially resonant in urban areas of the second-century Roman Empire because of the established adoptive imperial ideology. The long chain of 'good and adoptive emperors' (96–180 CE) led to a concomitant political ideology of meritocratic succession that praised father-son relations. This worldview provides a reasonable basis for explaining why adoptionistic Christologies were, in the words of one scholar, 'mostly a Roman affair.'"

61. Frede, "The Case for Pagan Monotheism," 81. On Galen and the Theodotians, see Peter Lampe, *From Paul to Valentinius: Christians at Rome in the First Two Centuries*, trans. Michael Steinhauser (London: Continuum, 2003), 345–48.

Conclusion

In this volume we have questioned the repeated claim that the earliest Christology in Jewish Christianity was adoptionist. We have seen that this assertion is unsubstantiated. Early creedal formulas (Rom 1:3–4) and fragments of apostolic preaching (Acts 2:36) do not exhibit features of adoptionist Christology. Mark's baptismal scene (Mark 1:9–11)—if taken in isolation from its literary context by someone familiar with Roman adoption practices and the deification of emperors—might conceivably be read as an adoption to divine sonship. However, it is very unlikely that this was Mark's intention given the overall shape of his Christology. The Shepherd of Hermas has a complicated and incoherent Christology that majors on the angelic-likeness of Christ rather than on his divine sonship. The Ebionites may have had some hints of adoptionism. Yet, it is thoroughly compressed into their wider framework of possession Christology and exaltation of the man Jesus. Even Theodotus the leatherworker does not appear to be an adoptionist, instead identifying Jesus as an inspired prophet. The later Theodotians can be divided into Melchizedekians and those who were fully fledged adoptionists. Of course, that was not the end of adoptionism. The view continued to manifest in various ways in the succeeding centuries, most prominently in the views of Paul of Samosata (ca. 200–275 CE), who was bishop of Antioch under Queen Zenobia of Palmyra. Paul believed that Jesus was a human being who became inhabited by the Logos, God's divine dynamic power, and the more Jesus was obedient to God's will, the more his soul achieved complete union with the Logos and attained divine status.[62] Unsurprisingly, Paul was condemned at the Council of Antioch in 268 CE when it was made clear that the personal Word took on flesh and was not merely an impersonal utterance finding subsistence in a human form.

62. Eusebius, *Hist. Eccl.* 7.27.2; Epiphanius, *Pan.* 65.1.5–8; Athanasius, *Syn.* 45.

CHAPTER 6

Adoptionism Then and Now

If the preceding study is correct, then there is no tangible evidence for an adoptionist Christology in the New Testament, nor in the Shepherd of Hermas, nor among the Ebionites, and it is not until we come across a group of Theodotians that we detect a full-blown adoptionism. What is stressed in the New Testament is not adoption, but enthronement: the Davidic Messiah is exalted to heavenly glory and divine regency. Concurrent with this was the widespread conviction that Jesus is the eschatological ruler of Ps 110:1 and identifiable with Israel's κύριος. When Davidic exaltation and divine identity are married together, divine sonship is necessarily intrinsic to Jesus rather than acquired by Jesus at a later point. Lest I be understood as overstating my case, there was diversity of Christologies in the early church, and we do find intimations of ideas that later became core tenets of belief among later adherents to monarchian and subordinationist Christologies. However, a fully orbed adoptionism emerged relatively late on the scene and was not one of the earliest Christologies.

Fast-forwarding a number of centuries, in the last two hundred years adoptionism has had something of a resurgence among rationalist or "old liberal" theologies, especially in Germany. The liberal Christology of the late nineteenth and early twentieth centuries was little more than an exposition of Friedrich Schleiermacher's comment that, "As certainly as Christ was a man, there must reside in human nature the possibility of taking up the divine into itself, just as did happen to

Jesus."[1] Not only that, but forms of adoptionism also continue to per-
sist in our contemporary age.[2] Yet I would be prepared to argue that
modern incarnations of adoptionism are inadequate articulations of
the person of Jesus Christ.

John Knox regarded the primitive adoptionism of the early church as
entirely adequate to say everything that needed to be said about Christ.[3]
Of course, Knox admits that it is impossible to plot a path back to that
point since the church's creedal ship has already sailed to kenotic and incarnational harbors. Even so, he surmises that given the alleged logical
impossibility of reconciling Jesus's personal pre-existence with his full
humanity, as well as the incredulity and unintelligibility of Trinitarian
metaphysics—not a mystery but a contradiction based on pious error and
confusion—Christian confessions must be reinterpreted. In such a rein-
terpretation, Jesus is no longer identified as one of the "persons" of the
Trinity, his pre-existence is limited to the divine purpose for his life, and
his divinity is reduced to the divine redemptive action achieved in his human life.[4] Knox says of Jesus: "He was not divested of his humanity, but his
humanity itself became a divine, and divinely redeeming, thing."[5] Knox's
view became very popular and shaped large swaths of modern Christology. The problem with Knox's narrative about the origins of Christology is that we have already found reason to contest whether adoptionist
Christology was the earliest articulation of Jesus's divine identity. Some
texts (e.g., Mark 1:11; Acts 2:36; Rom 1:3–4)—when read in isolation from
their literary context by those immersed in the imperial cult or by those
who hold to a view of divine simplicity where God's being can have no
becoming—could well end up reading these texts in an adoptionist sense.
However, as we have seen, adoptionism was hardly possible from within
the Jewish milieu that posited a sharp distinction between God the Creator
and his creation. Adoptionism was hardly intended by early authors like

---

1. Friedrich Schleiermacher, *The Christian Faith*, ed. H. R. Mackintosh and J. S.
Stewart (London: T&T Clark, 1999), 64.

2. See recently Charles Lee Irons, Danny André Dixon, and Dustin R. Smith, *The
Son of God: Three Views of the Identity of Jesus* (Eugene, OR: Wipf & Stock, 2015).

3. Knox, *Humanity and Divinity of Christ*, 58–60, 97–98.

4. Knox, *Humanity and Divinity of Christ*, 98–116.

5. Knox, *Humanity and Divinity of Christ*, 111.

Paul, Mark, and Luke. Furthermore, adoptionism lacks coherence when set beside the New Testament's overall witness to an incarnational Christology where the pre-existent Son is enfleshed as a human being, the man Jesus of Nazareth. In other words, adoptionism only really works within a particular Greco-Roman situation. It does not sit safely within a broadly Jewish view of divine ontology, and it requires either a heavily narrowed or hastily redacted canon from which to draw in order to fly. But that has not stopped others from dusting it off and trying to make it fly anew.

The British theologian John Macquarrie tried to hold adoptionism (or deification) and incarnationalism (or inhumanization) together in a dialectical tension. He maintained that these two models were not in an implacable conflict as each one needed the other for a full account of Jesus's person.[6] Macquarrie himself preferred to give priority to deification, the raising of a man toward God, in order to guard Jesus's humanity, something he saw as woefully neglected.[7] Despite Macquarrie's protests to the contrary,[8] he does appear to operate in an adoptionist orbit.[9] Macquarrie appeals to Paul's words, "All this is from God" (2 Cor 5:18), as a summary of the Jesus story, in order to ensure that adoptionism would only be half of the story.[10] The problem is that this is clearly an inadequate safeguard against a near total adoptionism as it is too vague a description of the divine element of Jesus's person. These inadequacies become clearer when Macquarrie declares that the driving question in christological enquiry is not "How does the Word assume humanity?" but "How does God become man?" The latter sets him on an adoptionist trajectory without much reservation.[11] If that were not clear enough, Macquarrie also sees the pres-

---

6. John Macquarrie, *Jesus Christ in Modern Thought* (London: SCM, 1990), 373.

7. Macquarrie, *Jesus Christ in Modern Thought*, 375–81.

8. Macquarrie, *Jesus Christ in Modern Thought*, 373, 382–83; John Macquarrie, *Christology Revisited* (Harrisburg, PA: Trinity Press, 1998), 23; John Macquarrie, *Stubborn Theological Questions* (London: SCM, 2003), 151.

9. See esp. Charles C. Helfing, "Reviving Adamic Adoptionism: The Example of John Macquarrie," *Theological Studies* 52 (1991): 476–94; Paul D. Molnar, *Incarnation and Resurrection: Toward a Contemporary Understanding* (Grand Rapids: Eerdmans, 2007), 359; Vernon L. Purdy, *The Christology of John Macquarrie* (New York: Peter Lang, 2009), 170–71.

10. Macquarrie, *Jesus Christ in Modern Thought*, 373.

11. Macquarrie, *Jesus Christ in Modern Thought*, 360.

ence of God in the man Jesus as something subsequent to his human birth and, furthermore, that Jesus's *hypostasis* ("person") was not the hypostasis of the divine Logos, but was a human *hypostasis* merely transfigured by immersion in the Holy Spirit. While Macquarrie's concern is for a more adequate recognition of the full humanity of Jesus, even so, his articulation of the incarnation avoids a clear identification between Jesus and God. That is because he makes Jesus's divinity a function of immersion in the Spirit rather than the union of the Logos with a human subject. Macquarrie is unable to acknowledge that Jesus is the Word of God incarnate simply because he is so.[12]

One school of advocates of Spirit-Christology stress Jesus's anointing with the Spirit as constituting the source of his divine nature, rather than relying on the hypostatic union of his human nature with the divine Logos as the source of his divinity. In that case, Jesus's divinity is not that of a divine person, but merely a model of divine presence and activity.[13] Another school of Spirit-Christology seeks to retain classical Trinitarian theism but argues for the necessity of the Spirit for the Son's identity and the vital role of the Spirit in the Son's incarnate life. Therefore, the Son is pre-existent, but hypostatic union is contingent on the bestowal of the Spirit upon Jesus.[14] The first species of Spirit-Christology is explicitly and proudly adoptionistic, while the second species remains vulnerable to the charge if several qualifications are not made. For instance, David Coffey has alleged that Mark revised an earlier Christology in which Jesus's divine sonship is derived from the resurrection, and situated it instead at Jesus's baptism, so that: "[T]he bestowal of the Spirit brings about the divine sonship of Jesus. The bestowal of the Spirit enters into the very constitution of his divine sonship."[15] Such a quotation is indicative of an approach that

12. Macquarrie, *Christology Revisited*, 61, 66–67, 76–79.

13. See, e.g., James P. MacKay, *Jesus, the Man and the Myth: A Contemporary Christology* (London: SCM, 1979).

14. See, e.g., David Coffey, *Grace: The Gift of the Spirit* (Milwaukee; Marquette University Press, 1997); David Coffey, *Deus Trinitas: The Doctrine of the Triune God* (New York: Oxford University Press, 1999); Ralph Del Colle, *Christ and the Spirit: Spirit-Christology in Trinitarian Perspective* (Oxford: Oxford University Press, 1994).

15. David Coffey, "The Holy Spirit as the Mutual Love of the Father and the Son," *TS* 51 (1990): 203.

certainly lends itself to a charge of adoptionism as it leaves open the question of whether Jesus was divine prior to receiving the Spirit or not. The result endangers the Logos's full personhood within Jesus.[16] Thankfully, more recent advocates of Spirit-Christology have taken these critiques seriously and see Spirit-Christology as a complement to classical Logos Christology.[17]

Various modern theologians have pointed out the shortcomings of adoptionism. I do not wish to rehearse their views here.[18] Suffice to say, my own reservations about adoptionism, apart from its lack of scriptural warrant, primarily concern what it entails about the economy of salvation.

First, modern adoptionists fall foul of Athanasius's axiom that one created being cannot redeem another created being. A purely human Jesus who becomes divine can be an immortalized teacher who lives anew in the continued promulgation of his philosophy, an angel-morphized sage who might pop down to earth to impart much needed advice to worthy inquirers, or a virtuous king who was voted celestial honors and thereafter bestows good fortune on suppliants who offer sacrifices upon his altar. But such a Jesus cannot be the Savior of humanity in the sense of reconciling them to God as Nicene Christianity has normally claimed.[19] In the end, the church's testimony is that only a fully divine

16. See Paul D. Molnar, "Deus Trinitas: Some Dogmatic Implications of David Coffey's Biblical Approach to the Trinity," *ITQ* 67 (2002): 36; Paul D. Molnar, "Response to David Coffey," *ITQ* 68 (2003): 65. See wider discussion about Spirit-Christology and adoptionism in Telford C. Work, "Jesus' New Relationship with the Holy Spirit, and Ours: How Biblical-Spirit Christology Helps Resolve a Chalcedonian Dilemma," in *Christology: Ancient and Modern*, ed. O. D. Crisp and F. Sanders (Grand Rapids: Zondervan, 2013), 179–80; Gregory J. Liston, *The Anointed Church: Toward a Third Article Christology* (Minneapolis: Fortress, 2015), 197–203, 344–45.

17. See e.g., Amos Yong, *The Spirit Poured Out on All Flesh: Pentecostalism and the Possibility of Global Theology* (Grand Rapids: Baker, 2005), 110–11; Myk Habets, *The Anointed Son: A Trinitarian Spirit Christology*, Princeton Theological Monograph Series (Eugene, OR: Pickwick, 2010), 5, 19–20.

18. See e.g., Thomas F. Torrance, *Incarnation: The Person and Life of Christ* (Downers Grove, IL: InterVarsity, 2008), 229; Oliver D. Crisp, *Divinity and Humanity: The Incarnation Reconsidered* (Cambridge: CUP, 2007), 26.

19. Athanasius, *C. Ar.* 2.67: "If being a creature, he (the Son) had become human, humanity would have remained just as it was, not joined to God" (Newman and Rob-

and fully human Jesus can be a mediator (1 Tim 2:5), a great high priest (Heb 4:14), "Immanuel" (Matt 1:23), the "Word made flesh" (John 1:14), a "great God and Savior" (Tit 2:5), who has "union with God and with you" (Ign. *Smyrn*. 12.2), who "became what we are, so that we might become what he is" (Irenaeus, *Haer*. 5, praef.). We can only say God is *for us* if God is *with us*; and we can only say God is *with us* if God was *one of us*. Salvation is attained in Christ and by Christ in his double redemptive movement of God descending toward humanity and then lifting humanity up to God.

Second, adoptionism contends that Jesus became the Son of God by merit and thus promotes a type of merit theology where our own status and salvation is by works. Justo L. González argues that modern adoptionism denies the embodiment and efficacy of grace in Jesus Christ in favor of the view that Jesus merited divine favor by his good works. Jesus becomes the paragon of virtue who is rewarded with divine honors. Viewed this way, adoptionism is the counterpart to the American myth that all people have a chance to make it on the back of their own hard work and on the steam of their own effort. González writes, "Jesus Christ must be more than the first among the redeemed, more than the local boy who makes good. He must also be the Redeemer, the power from outside who breaks into our closed reality and breaks its structures of oppression. He must be more than the 'adopted Son of God.' He must be God adopting us as sons and daughters."[20]

---

ertson, *NPNF*²). Note also Irenaeus, *Haer*. 3.19.1: "For it was for this end that the Word of God was made man, and He who was the Son of God became the Son of man, that man, having been taken into the Word, and receiving the adoption, might become the son of God. For by no other means could we have attained to incorruptibility and immortality, unless we had been united to incorruptibility and immortality. But how could we be joined to incorruptibility and immortality, unless, first, incorruptibility and immortality had become that which we also are, so that the corruptible might be swallowed up by incorruptibility, and the mortal by immortality, that we might receive the adoption of sons?" (Roberts and Rambaut, *ANF*) and Irenaeus, *Haer*. 4.33.4 "How can they be saved unless it was God who wrought their salvation upon earth? Or how shall a human pass into God, unless God first passed into a human?" (Roberts and Rambaut, *ANF*).

20. Justo L. González, *Manana: Christian Theology from a Hispanic Perspective* (Nashville: Abingdon, 1990), 144–45.

A Christology that presents us with a mere man who bids us to earn our salvation is an impoverished alternative to the God of grace and mercy who took on our flesh and "became sin" so that we might become the "righteousness of God." I prefer a Christology where the Son was crucified on the cross for us, was glorified in the resurrection for us, and was exalted to heaven for us—so that on the appointed day, we all would attain adoption as children of God and the redemption of our bodies in the new creation.

Bibliography

Adams, Sean A., and Seth M. Ehorn. "What Is a Composite Citation? An Introduction." Pages 1–16 in *Composite Citations in Antiquity*. Vol. 1: *Jewish, Graeco-Roman, and Early Christian Uses*. Edited by Sean A. Adams and Seth M. Ehorn. LNTS 525. London: Bloomsbury, 2016.

Ahearne-Kroll, Stephen P. "The Scripturally Complex Presentation of Jesus in the Gospel of Mark." Pages 46–68 in *Portraits of Jesus: Studies in Christology*. Edited by Susan E. Meyers. WUNT 2.321. Tübingen: Mohr Siebeck, 2012.

The Ante-Nicene Fathers. Edited by Alexander Roberts and James Donaldson. 1885–1887. 10 vols. Reprint. Peabody, MA: Hendrickson, 1994.

The Apostolic Fathers in English. Translated by Rick Brannan. Lexham Press, 2012.

Balabanski, Victoria. *Eschatology in the Making: Mark, Matthew and the Didache*. SNTSMS 97. Cambridge: Cambridge University Press, 2005.

Barrett, C. K. *A Critical and Exegetical Commentary on the Acts of the Apostles*. 2 vols. ICC. Edinburgh: T&T Clark, 1994.

Bauckham, Richard. *Jesus and the God of Israel: God Crucified and Other Studies on the New Testament's Christology of Divine Identity*. Grand Rapids: Eerdmans, 2009.

———. "The Origin of the Ebionites." Pages 162–81 in *The Image of the Judaeo-Christians in Ancient Jewish and Christian Literature*. Edited by Peter J. Tomson and Doris Lambers-Petry. WUNT 158. Tübingen: Mohr Siebeck, 2003.

———. "Paul's Christology of Divine Identity." In *Oxford Handbook of Pauline Studies*. Edited by R. Barry Matlock. Oxford: Oxford University Press, forthcoming.

———. "The Throne of God and the Worship of Jesus." Pages 43–69 in *The Jewish Roots of Christological Monotheism*. Edited by Carey C. Newman, James R. Davila, and Gladys S. Lewis. JSJSup 63. Leiden: Brill, 1999.

Bates, Matthew W. *The Birth of the Trinity: Jesus, God, and Spirit in New Testament and Early Christian Interpretations of the Old Testament.* Oxford: Oxford University Press, 2015.

———. "A Christology of Incarnation and Enthronement: Romans 1:3–4 as Unified, Nonadoptionist, and Nonconciliatory." *CBQ* 77 (2015): 107–27.

Beard, Mary. *The Roman Triumph.* London: Belknap, 2009.

Beard, Mary, John North, and Simon Price. *Religions of Rome.* 2 vols. Cambridge: Cambridge University Press, 1998.

Beasley-Murray, Paul. "Romans 1:3f: An Early Confession of Faith in the Lordship of Jesus." *TynBul* 31 (1980): 147–54.

Bernett, Monika. *Der Kaiserkult in Judaä unter den Herodiern und Römern: Untersuchungen zur politischen und religiösen Geschicht Judaäs von 30 v. bis 66 n. Chr.* WUNT 203. Tübingen: Mohr Siebeck, 2007.

Bird, Michael F. *Are You the One Who Is to Come? The Historical Jesus and the Messianic Question.* Grand Rapids: Baker, 2007.

———. "Did Jesus Think He Was God?" Pages 45–70 in *How God Became Jesus.* Edited by Michael F. Bird. Grand Rapids: Zondervan, 2014.

———. *Jesus Is the Christ: The Messianic Testimony of the Gospels.* Downers Grove, IL: IVP, 2012.

———. *Romans.* The Story of God Bible Commentary. Grand Rapids: Zondervan, 2016.

Blomberg, Craig L. *From Pentecost to Patmos: Acts to Revelation. An Introduction and Survey.* Nottingham: Apollos, 2006.

Boring, M. Eugene. *Mark: A Commentary.* New Testament Library. Louisville: Westminster John Knox, 2006.

———. "Markan Christology: God-Language for Jesus? *NTS* 45 (1999): 451–71.

Boring, M. Eugene, Klaus Berger, and Carsten Colpe, eds. *Hellenistic Commentary to the New Testament.* Nashville: Abingdon, 1995.

Bousset, Wilhelm. *Kyrios Christos: A History of the Belief in Christ from the Beginnings of Christianity to Irenaeus.* Translated by John E. Steely. Waco, TX: Baylor University Press, 2013.

Brown, Harold O. J. *Heresies.* New York: Doubleday, 1984.

Brown, Raymond E. *The Birth of the Messiah.* Garden City, NY: Doubleday, 1977.

———. *An Introduction to New Testament Christology.* New York: Paulist, 1984.

Bryan, Christopher. *The Resurrection of the Messiah.* New York: Oxford University Press, 2011.

Buckwalter, Douglas. *The Character and Purpose of Luke's Christology.* SNTSMS 89. Cambridge: Cambridge University Press, 1996.

Bultmann, Rudolf. *Theology of the New Testament.* 2 vols. London: SCM, 1952.

Calhoun, Robert Matthew. *Paul's Definition of the Gospel in Romans 1.* WUNT 2.316. Tübingen: Mohr Siebeck, 2011.

Campbell, Constantine R. *Basics of Verbal Aspect in Biblical Greek*. Grand Rapids: Zondervan, 2008.

Casey, Maurice. *From Jewish Prophet to Gentile God: The Origins and Development of New Testament Christology*. Cambridge: James Clarke & Co., 1991.

Cavadini, John C. *The Last Christology of the West: Adoptionism in Spain and Gaul, 785–820*. Philadelphia: University of Philadelphia Press, 1993.

Chandler, C. "Heresy and Empire: The Role of the Adoptionist Controversy in Charlemagne's Conquest of the Spanish March." *IHR* 24 (2002): 505–27.

Chester, Andrew. *Deus Trinitas: The Doctrine of the Triune God*. New York: Oxford University Press, 1999.

———. *Grace: The Gift of the Spirit*. Milwaukee: Marquette University Press, 1997.

———. "High Christology—Whence, When and Why?" *Early Christianity* 2 (2011): 22–50.

———. *Messiah and Exaltation: Jewish Messianic and Visionary Traditions and New Testament Christology*. WUNT 207. Tübingen: Mohr Siebeck, 2007.

Coffey, David. "The Holy Spirit as the Mutual Love of the Father and the Son." *TS* 51 (1990): 193–229.

Cole, Spencer. *Cicero and the Rise of Deification at Rome*. Cambridge: Cambridge University Press, 2013.

Colle, Ralph Del. *Christ and the Spirit: Spirit-Christology in Trinitarian Perspective*. Oxford: Oxford University Press, 1994.

Collins, Adela Y. *Mark*. Hermeneia. Minneapolis: Fortress, 2007.

———. "Mark and His Readers: The Son of God among Greeks and Romans." *HTR* 93 (2000): 85–100.

———. "Mark and His Readers: The Son of God among Jews." *HTR* 92 (1999): 393–408.

———. "The Worship of Jesus and the Imperial Cult." Pages 234–57 in *The Jewish Roots of Christological Monotheism: Papers from the St. Andrews Conference on the Historical Origins of the Worship of Jesus*. Edited by Carey C. Newman, James R. Davila, and Gladys S. Lewis. JSJSup 63. Leiden: Brill, 1999.

Collins, Adela Y., and John J. Collins. *King as Messiah and Son of God: Divine, Human, and Angelic Messianic Figures in Biblical and Related Literature*. Grand Rapids: Eerdmans, 2008.

Collins, John J. "Jewish Monotheism and Christian Theology." Pages 81–105 in *Aspects of Monotheism: How God is One*. Edited by Hershel Shanks and Jack Meinhardt. Washington, DC: Biblical Archaeology Society, 1997.

Cranfield, C. E. B. *The Epistle to the Romans*. 2 vols. ICC. Edinburgh: T&T Clark, 1975–1979.

Crisp, Oliver D. *Divinity and Humanity: The Incarnation Reconsidered*. Cambridge: Cambridge University Press, 2007.

Cullmann, Oscar. *The Christology of the New Testament*. Philadelphia: Westminster John Knox, 1959.

Danker, Frederick W., Walter Bauer, William F. Arndt, and F. Wilbur Gingrich. *Greek-English Lexicon of the New Testament and Other Early Christian Literature*. 3rd ed. Chicago: University Press, 2000.

Davis, Philip G. "Mark's Christological Paradox." Pages 163–77 in *The Synoptic Gospels: A Sheffield Reader*. Edited by Craig A. Evans and Stanley E Porter. Sheffield: Sheffield Academic Press, 1995.

Deissmann, Adolf. *Light from the Ancient East: The New Testament Illustrated by Recently Discovered Texts of the Graeco-Roman World*. Translated by Lionel R. M. Strachan. London: Hodder & Stoughton, 1910.

Dunn, James D. G. *Beginning from Jerusalem*. Volume 2 of *Christianity in the Making*. Grand Rapids: Eerdmans, 2009.

———. *Christology in the Making: A New Testament Inquiry into the Origins of the Doctrine of the Incarnation*. 2nd ed. London: SCM, 1986.

———. *Did the First Christians Worship Jesus? The New Testament Evidence*. London: SPCK, 2010.

———. *Romans*. 2 vols. WBC. Dallas, TX: Word, 1988.

———. *Unity and Diversity in the New Testament: An Inquiry into the Character of Earliest Christianity*. 3rd ed. London: SCM, 2006.

Ehrman, Bart D. *How Jesus Became God: The Exaltation of a Jewish Preacher from Galilee*. New York: HarperOne, 2014.

———. *Lost Christianities: The Battles for Scripture and the Faiths We Never Knew*. Oxford: Oxford University Press, 2003.

———. *The New Testament: A Historical Introduction to the Early Christian Writings*. 4th ed. Oxford: Oxford University Press, 2008.

Ehrman, Bart D., and Zlatko Pleše. *The Apocryphal Gospels: Texts and Translations*. Oxford: Oxford University Press, 2011.

Epiphanius. *The Panarion of Epiphanius of Salamis, Book I (Sects 1–46)*. Translated by Frank Williams. Nag Hammadi and Manichaean Studies 63. Leiden: Brill, 2009.

Eskola, Timo. *Messiah and the Throne*. WUNT 2.142; Tübingen: Mohr Siebeck, 2001.

Evans, Craig A. *Mark 8:27–16:20*. WBC 34b. Nashville: Nelson, 2001.

Fee, Gordon D. *Pauline Christology: An Exegetical-Theological Study*. Peabody, MA: Hendrickson, 2007.

Fletcher-Louis, Crispin H. T. "Jesus as the High Priestly Messiah: Part 2." *JSHJ* 5 (2007): 57–79.

———. *Jesus Monotheism*. Vol. 1. of *Christological Origins: The Emerging Consensus and Beyond*. Eugene, OR: Wipf & Stock, 2015.

———. *Luke-Acts: Angels, Christology, and Soteriology*. WUNT 2.94. Tübingen: Mohr Siebeck, 1997.

France, R. T. *The Gospel of Mark: A Commentary on the Greek Text*. Grand Rapids: Eerdmans, 2002.

Frede, Michael. "The Case for Pagan Monotheism." Pages 53–81 in *One God: Pagan Monotheism in the Roman Empire*. Edited by Stephen Mitchell and Peter Van Nuffelen. Cambridge: Cambridge University Press, 2010.

Fredriksen, Paula. *From Jesus to Christ: The Origins of the New Testament Images of Jesus*. New Haven: Yale University Press, 1988.

———. "Mandatory Retirement: Ideas in the Study of Christian Origins Whose Time Has Come to Go." Pages 25–38 in *Israel's God and Rebecca's Children: Christology and Community in Early Judaism and Christianity. Essays in Honor of Larry W. Hurtado and Alan F. Segal*. Edited by David B. Capes, April D. De-Conick, Helen K Bond, and Troy A. Miller. Waco, TX: Baylor University Press, 2007.

Garland, David E. *A Theology of Mark's Gospel*. Biblical Theology of the New Testament. Grand Rapids: Zondervan, 2015.

Garnsey, Peter, and Richard P. Saller. *The Roman Empire: Economy, Society and Culture*. London: Duckworth, 1987.

Gathercole, Simon J. *The Gospel of Judas*. Oxford: Oxford University Press, 2007.

———. *The Pre-existent Son: Recovering the Christologies of Matthew, Mark, and Luke*. Grand Rapids: Eerdmans, 2006.

———. "What Did the First Christians Think about Jesus?" Pages 94–116 in *How God Became Jesus: The Real Origins of Belief in Jesus' Divine Nature*. Edited by Michael F. Bird. Grand Rapids: Zondervan, 2014.

Geddert, Timothy J. "The Implied YHWH Christology of Mark's Gospel: Mark's Challenge to the Readers to 'Connect the Dots.'" *BBR* 25 (2015): 325–40.

González, Justo L. *Manana: Christian Theology from a Hispanic Perspective*. Nashville: Abingdon, 1990.

González, Justo L., and Catherine Gunsalus González. *Heretics for Armchair Theologians*. Louisville: Westminster John Knox, 2008.

Goulder, Michael D. "A Poor Man's Christology." *NTS* 45 (1999): 332–48.

Gradel, Ittai. *Emperor Worship and Roman Religion*. Oxford: Clarendon, 2002.

Grillmeier, Alois, and Theresia Hainthaler. *Jesus der Christus im Glauben der Kirche. I. Von der Apostolischen Zeit bis zum Konzil von Chalcedon (451)*. Freiburg im Breisgau: Herder, 1979.

Gundry, Robert H. *Mark: A Commentary on His Apology for the Cross*. Grand Rapids: Eerdmans, 1993.

Gunton, Colin E. *Yesterday & Today: A Study in Continuity in Christology*. London: SPCK, 1997.

Habets, Myk. *The Anointed Son: A Trinitarian Spirit Christology*. Princeton Theological Monograph Series 129. Eugene, OR: Pickwick, 2010.

Hägerland, Tobias. *Jesus and the Forgiveness of Sins: An Aspect of His Prophetic Mission*. SNTSMS 150. Cambridge: Cambridge University Press, 2012.

Häkkinen, Sakari. "Ebionites." Pages 247–78 in *A Companion to Second-Century*

Christian "Heretics." Edited by Antti Marjanen and Petri Luomanen. VCSup 76. Leiden: Brill, 2005.

Hatina, Thomas R. "Embedded Scripture Texts and the Plurality of Meaning: The Announcement of the 'Voice from Heaven' In Mark 1.11 as a Case Study." Pages 81–99 in *Biblical Interpretation in Early Christian Gospels.* Vol. 1: *The Gospel of Mark.* Edited by Thomas R. Hatina. LNTS 304. London: T&T Clark, 2006.

Hays, Richard B. *Reading Backwards: Figural Christology and the Fourfold Gospel Witness.* Waco, TX: Baylor University Press, 2014.

Helfing, Charles C. "Reviving Adamic Adoptionism: The Example of John Macquarrie." *TS* 52 (1991): 476–94.

Hengel, Martin. "Christological Titles in Early Christianity." Pages 425–48 in *The Messiah.* Edited by James H. Charlesworth. Minneapolis: Fortress, 1992.

———. *Son of God: The Origin of Christology and the History of Jewish-Hellenistic Religion.* Translated by John Bowden. Philadelphia: Fortress Press, 1976.

———. *Studies in Early Christology.* Edinburgh: T&T Clark, 1995.

Henrichs-Tarasenkova, Nina. *Luke's Christology of Divine Identity.* LNTS 542. London: T&T Clark, 2016.

Hill, Charles E. "An Exclusive Religion: Orthodoxy and Heresy, Inclusion and Exclusion." Pages 151–68 in *How God Became Jesus: The Real Origins of Belief in Jesus' Divine Nature.* Edited by Michael F. Bird. Grand Rapids: Zondervan, 2014.

Hill, William J. *The Three-Personed God: The Trinity as the Mystery of Salvation.* Washington, DC: Catholic University of America, 1982.

Holmes, Michael W. *The Apostolic Fathers: Greek Texts and English Translations.* 3rd ed. Grand Rapids: BakerAcademic, 2007.

Hurtado, Larry W. "'Ancient Jewish Monotheism' in the Hellenistic and Roman Periods." *JAJ* 4 (2013): 379–400.

———. "First-Century Jewish Monotheism." *JSNT* 71 (1998): 3–26.

———. *Lord Jesus Christ: Devotion to Jesus in Earliest Christianity.* Grand Rapids: Eerdmans, 2003.

———. "Monotheism, Principal Angels, and the Background of Christology." Pages 546–64 in *The Oxford Handbook of the Dead Sea Scrolls.* Edited by Timothy H. Lim and John J. Collins. Oxford: Oxford University Press, 2010.

———. *One God, One Lord: Early Christian Devotion and Ancient Jewish Monotheism.* Philadelphia: Fortress Press, 1988.

Irons, Charles Lee., Danny André Dixon, and Dustin R. Smith. *The Son of God: Three Views of the Identity of Jesus.* Eugene, OR: Wipf & Stock, 2015.

Janse, Sam. *"You Are My Son": The Reception History of Psalm 2 in Early Judaism and the Early Church.* Leuven: Peeters, 2009.

Jewett, Robert. "The Redaction and Use of an Early Christian Confession in Romans 1:3–4." Pages 99–122 in *The Living Text: Essays in Honor of Ernest W.*

Saunders. Edited by Dennis E. Groh and Robert Jewett. New York: University Press of America, 1985.

Jipp, Joshua W. "Ancient, Modern, and Future Interpretations of Romans 1:3–4: Reception History and Biblical Interpretation." *JTI* 3 (2009): 227–45.

———. *Christ is King: Paul's Royal Ideology*. Minneapolis: Fortress, 2015.

Johansson, Daniel. "*Kyrios* in the Gospel of Mark." *JSNT* 33 (2010): 101–24.

———. "'Who Can Forgive Sins but God Alone?' Human and Angelic Agents, and Divine Forgiveness in Early Judaism." *JSNT* 33 (2011): 351–74.

Johnson, Luke Timothy. *Religious Experience in Earliest Christianity: A Missing Dimension in New Testament Study*. Minneapolis: Fortress, 1998.

———. Review of *No One Seeks for God: An Exegetical and Theological Study of Romans 1:18–3:20*, by Richard H. Bell. *RBL* (1999).

Josephus, Flavius. *Against Apion*. Vol. 10 of *Flavius Josephus: Translation and Commentary*. Edited by Steve Mason. Translation and commentary by John M. G. Barclay. Leiden: Brill, 2007.

Käsemann, Ernst. "The Canon of the New Testament and the Unity of the Church." Pages 95–223 in *Essays on New Testament Themes*. SBT 41. London: SCM, 1964.

Kee, Howard Clark. "Christology in Mark's Gospel." Pages 187–208 in *Judaism and Their Messiahs at the Turn of the Christian Era*. Edited by Jacob Neusner, William Scott Green, and Ernest S. Frerichs. Cambridge: Cambridge University Press, 1987.

Keener, Craig. *Acts: An Exegetical Commentary*. 4 vols. Grand Rapids: Baker, 2012–2015.

Kelly, J. N. D. *Early Christian Doctrines*. 5th ed. London: Continuum, 2001.

Kirk, J. R. Daniel. *A Man Attested by God: The Human Jesus of the Synoptic Gospels*. Grand Rapids: Eerdmans, 2016.

———. *Unlocking Romans: Resurrection and the Justification of God*. Grand Rapids: Eerdmans, 2008.

Kirk, J. R. Daniel, and Stephen L. Young. "I Will Set His Hand to the Sea: Psalm 86:28 (LXX) and Christology in Mark." *JBL* 133 (2014): 333–40.

Klijn, Albertus F. J., and G. J. Reinink. *Patristic Evidence for Jewish-Christian Sects*. NovTSup 36. Leiden: Brill, 1973.

Knox, John. *The Church and the Reality of Christ*. London: Collins, 1963

———. *The Humanity and Divinity of Christ: A Study of Pattern in Christology*. Cambridge: Cambridge University Press, 1967.

Kok, Michael J. *The Gospel on the Margins: The Reception of Mark in the Second Century*. Minneapolis: Fortress, 2015.

Lampe, Peter. *From Paul to Valentinius: Christians at Rome in the First Two Centuries*. Translated by Michael Steinhauser; London: Continuum, 2003.

Lee, Aquila H. I. *From Messiah to Preexistent Son*. Eugene, OR: Wipf & Stock, 2005.

Leim, Joshua E. "In the Glory of the Father: Intertextuality and the Apocalyptic Son of Man in the Gospel of Mark." *JTI* 7 (2013): 213–32.

Liston, Gregory J. *The Anointed Church: Toward a Third Article Christology*. Minneapolis: Fortress, 2015.

Litwa, M. David. *Iesus Deus: The Early Christian Depiction of Jesus as a Mediterranean God*. Minneapolis: Fortress, 2014.

MacKay, James P. *Jesus, the Man and the Myth: A Contemporary Christology*. London: SCM, 1979.

Macquarrie, John. *Christology Revisited*. Harrisburg, PA: Trinity Press, 1998

———. *Jesus Christ in Modern Thought*. London: SCM, 1990.

Marcus, Joel. *Mark 1–8: A New Translation with Introduction and Commentary*. AB. New Haven. Yale University Press, 2000.

———. *Mark 8–16: A New Translation with Introduction and Commentary*. AB. New Haven: Yale University Press, 2007.

———. "Mark 14:61: 'Are You the Messiah-Son of God?'" *NovT* 31 (1989): 125–41.

———. *Stubborn Theological Questions*. London: SCM, 2003.

———. *The Way of the Lord: Christological Exegesis of the Old Testament in the Gospel of Mark*. Louisville: Westminster John Knox, 1992.

Marshall, I. Howard. *The Origins of New Testament Christology*. England, UK: InterVarsity, 1977.

Matera, Frank. *New Testament Christology*. Louisville: Westminster John Knox, 1999.

McDonough, Sean M. *Christ as Creator: Origins of a New Testament Doctrine*. Oxford: Oxford University Press, 2009.

McGrath, James F. *The Only True God: Early Christian Monotheism in its Jewish Context*. Urbana: University of Illinois Press, 2009.

Moberly, Walter. "How Appropriate is 'Monotheism' as a Category for Biblical Interpretation?" Pages 216–34 in *Early Jewish and Christian Monotheism*. Edited by Loren T. Stuckenbruck and Wendy E. S. North. JSNTSup 263. London: T&T Clark, 2004.

Molnar, Paul D. "*Deus Trinitas*: Some Dogmatic Implications of David Coffey's Biblical Approach to the Trinity." *ITQ* 67 (2002): 33–54.

———. *Incarnation and Resurrection: Toward a Contemporary Understanding*. Grand Rapids: Eerdmans, 2007.

———. "Response to David Coffey." *ITQ* 68 (2003): 61–65.

Morrison, Gregg S. *The Turning Point in the Gospel of Mark: A Study in Markan Christology*. Eugene, OR: Pickwick, 2015.

Naluparayil, Jacob Chacko. "Jesus of the Gospel of Mark: Present State of Research." *CurBS* 8 (2000): 191–226.

The Nicene and Post-Nicene Fathers. Series 1. Edited by Philip Schaff. 1886–1889. 14 vols. Reprint. Peabody, MA: Hendrickson, 1994.

The Nicene and Post-Nicene Fathers. Series 2. Edited by Philip Schaff. 1890–1900. 14 vols. Reprint. Peabody, MA: Hendrickson, 1994.

Old Testament Pseudepigrapha. Edited James H. Charlesworth. 2 vols. New York: Doubleday, 1983, 1985.

Olson, Duane. *Issues in Contemporary Christian Thought: A Fortress Introduction.* Minneapolis: Fortress, 2011.

Owen, Paul. "Jesus as God's Chief Agent in Mark's Christology." Pages 40–57 in *Mark, Manuscripts, and Monotheism. Essays in Honor of Larry W. Hurtado.* Edited by Chris Keith and Dieter T. Roth. LNTS 528. London: Bloomsbury, 2015.

Osiek, Caroline. *The Shepherd of Hermas.* Hermeneia. Minneapolis: Fortress, 1999.

Paget, James Carleton. "Jewish Christianity." Pages 731–75 in vol. 3 of *Cambridge History of Judaism.* Edited by William Horbury, W. D. Davies, and John Sturdy. Cambridge: Cambridge University Press, 2001.

Pannenberg, Wolfhart. *Jesus—God and Man.* Philadelphia: Westminster, 1968.

———. *Systematic Theology.* 3 vols. London: T&T Clark, 2004.

Papandrea, James L. *The Earliest Christologies: Five Images of Christ in the Postapostolic Age.* Downers Grove, IL: InterVarsity, 2016.

Pearson, Birger A., and Søren Giversen, "Melchizedek." Pages in 438–444 in *The Nag Hammadi Library in English.* Rev. ed. Edited by James M. Robinson. Leiden: Brill, 1988.

Peppard, Michael. *The Son of God in the Roman World: Divine Sonship in its Social and Political Context.* Oxford: Oxford University Press, 2011.

Pesch, Rudolf. *Apostelgeschichte.* 2 vols. EKKNT. Zurich: Neukirchener Verlage, 1986.

———. *Das Markusevangelium.* 2 vols. HThKNT. Freiburg im Breisgau: Herder, 1976–1977.

Pokorný, Petr. *The Genesis of Christology.* Edinburgh: T&T Clark, 1987.

Porter, Stanley E. "Further Comments on the Use of the Old Testament in the New Testament." Pages 98–110 in *The Intertextuality of the Epistles: Explorations in Theory and Practice.* Edited by Thomas L. Brodie, Dennis R. MacDonald, and Stanley E. Porter. New Testament Monographs 16. Sheffield: Sheffield Phoenix, 2007.

———. *Idioms of the Greek New Testament.* 2nd ed. Sheffield: Sheffield Academic Press, 1992.

Poythress, Vern S. "Is Romans 1:3–4 a Pauline Confession after All?" *ExpTim* 87 (1976): 180–83.

Purdy, Vernon L. *The Christology of John Macquarrie.* New York: Peter Lang, 2009.

Reasoner, Mark. *Roman Imperial Texts: A Sourcebook.* Minneapolis: Fortress, 2013.

Rowe, C. Kavin. *Early Narrative Christology: The Lord in the Gospel of Luke.* Grand Rapids: Baker, 2009.

Sandmel, Samuel. "Parallelomania," *JBL* 81 (1962): 1–13.

Schlier, Heinrich. "Zu Röm 1.3f." Pages 207–18 in *Neues Testament und Geschichte, Historisches Geschehen und Deutung im Neuen Testament. Oscar Cullmann zum*

70. Geburtstag. Edited by Heinrich Baltensweiler and Bo Reicke. Zürich: Theologischer Verlag, 1972.

Schleiermacher, Friedrich. *The Christian Faith*. Edited by H. R. Mackintosh and J. S. Stewart. London: T&T Clark, 1999.

Schmithals, Walter. *The Theology of the First Christians*. Translated by O. C. Dean Jr. Louisville: Westminster: John Knox, 1997.

Schröter, Jens. *From Jesus to the New Testament: Early Christian Theology and the Origin of the New Testament Canon*. Translated by Wayne Coppins. Waco, TX: Baylor University Press, 2013.

Scott, James M. *Adoption as Sons of God*. WUNT 2.48; Tübingen: Mohr Siebeck, 1992.

Segal, Alan. "Jewish Christianity." Pages 326–51 in *Eusebius, Christianity, and Judaism*. Edited by Harold W. Attridge and Gōhei Hata. Detroit: Wayne State University, 1992.

Skarsaune, Oskar. "The Ebionites." Pages 419–62 in *Jewish Believers in Jesus*. Edited by Oskar Skarsaune and Reidar Hvalvik. Peabody, MA: Hendrickson, 2007.

———. "Is Christianity Monotheistic? Patristic Perspectives on a Jewish-Christian Debate." *Studia Patristica* 29 (1997): 340–63.

Stuhlmacher Peter. *Biblische Theologie des Neuen Testaments*. 2 vols. Göttingen: Vandenhoeck & Ruprecht, 1992–1999.

Stuckenbruck, Loren T. *Angel Veneration and Christology: A Study in Early Judaism and in the Christology of the Apocalypse*. WUNT 2.70.Tübingen: Mohr Siebeck, 1995.

Talbert, Charles H. "The Development of Christology in the First 100 Years: A Modest Proposal." Pages 3–42 in *The Development of Christology During the First Hundred Years, and Other Essays on Early Christian Christology*. Leiden: Brill, 2011.

Tannehill, Robert. *The Narrative Unity of Luke–Acts: A Literary Interpretation*. 2 vols. Minneapolis: Fortress, 1986–1990.

Tilling, Chris. *Paul's Divine Christology*. Grand Rapids: Eerdmans, 2012.

Torrance, Thomas F. *Incarnation: The Person and Life of Christ*. Downers Grove, IL: InterVarsity, 2008.

Vielhauer, Paul. "Erwägungen Zur Christologie des Markus evangeliums." Pages 155–69 in *Zeit und Geschichte. Dankesgabe an Rudolf Bultmann zum 80. Geburtstag*. Edited by Erich Dinkler. Tübingen: Mohr Siebeck, 1964.

Watts, Rikki. *Isaiah's New Exodus and Mark*. WUNT 99. Tübingen: Mohr Siebeck, 1997.

Weiss, Johannes. *Earliest Christianity: A History of the Period AD 30–150*. 2 vols. New York: Harper, 1959.

Wellhausen, Julius. *Das Evangelium Marci*. Berlin: G. Reimer, 1903.

Wilckens, Ulrich. *Missionsreden der Apostelgeschichte: Form- und Traditionsge-*

schichtliche Untersuchungen. 3rd ed. WMANT 5. Zürich: Neurkirchenener Verlag, 1974.

Winter, Bruce W. *Divine Honours for the Caesars: The First Christians' Responses*. Grand Rapids: Eerdmans, 2015.

Witherington, Ben. "Jesus as the Alpha and Omega of New Testament Thought." Pages 25–46 in *Contours of Christology in the New Testament*. Edited by Richard N. Longenecker. Grand Rapids: Eerdmans, 2005.

Work, Telford C. "Jesus' New Relationship with the Holy Spirit, and Ours: How Biblical-Spirt Christology Helps Resolve a Chalcedonian Dilemma." Pages 179–80 in *Christology: Ancient and Modern*. Edited by Oliver D. Crisp and Fred Sanders. Grand Rapids: Zondervan, 2013.

White, John L. *The Apostle of God: Paul and the Promise of Abraham*. Peabody, MA: Hendrickson, 1999.

Whitenton, Michael R. *Hearing Kyriotic Sonship: A Cognitive and Rhetorical Approach to the Characterization of Mark's Jesus*. BibInt 148. Leiden: Brill, 2016.

Whitsett, Christopher G. "Son of God, Seed of David: Paul's Messianic Exegesis on Romans [1]:3–4." *JBL* 119 (2000): 661–81.

Wilhite, David E. *The Gospel according to Heretics: Discovering Orthodoxy through Early Christological Conflicts*. Grand Rapids: Baker, 2015.

Wright, N.T. *Jesus and the Victory of God*. Volume 2 of *Christian Origins and the Question of God*. London: SPCK, 1996.

———. *Paul and the Faithfulness of God*. Volume 4 of *Christian Origins and the Question of God*. London: SPCK, 2014.

———. *The Resurrection of the Son of God*. Volume 3 of *Christian Origins and the Question of God*. London: SPCK, 2003.

Yeago, David S. "The New Testament and Nicene Dogma: A Contribution to the Recovery of Theological Exegesis." Pages 87–100 in *Theological Interpretation of Scripture: Classic and Contemporary Readings*. Edited by Stephen E. Fowl. Malden, MA: Blackwell, 1997.

Yong, Amos. *The Spirit Poured Out on All Flesh: Pentecostalism and the Possibility of Global Theology*. Grand Rapids: Baker, 2005.

Zanker, Paul. *The Power of Images in the Age of Augustus*. Translated by Alan Shapiro. Ann Arbor: University of Michigan Press, 1988.

Index of Names and Subjects

Index of Ancient Sources